WHAT'S WRONG

WITH THE

CHRISTIAN RIGHT

What's
WRONG
WITH THE
CHRISTIAN
RIGHT

JAN G. LINN

What's Wrong With The Christian Right

Cover design: Bob Willbanks
Interior design: Lynne Condellone

BrownWalker Press
Boca Raton , Florida
USA • 2004

ISBN: 1-58112-424-4

BrownWalker.com

FOR DAVID POLK

CONTENTS

ACKNOWLEDGMENTS

I bear full responsibility for this book. That said, while writing it, I became more acutely aware of my dependence as an author on the encouragement, support, and suggestions of others.

Alice Lundy Blum's enthusiastic response after reading the first draft helped to rekindle my belief that this was a timely and important work to complete. Further, her suggestions added immensely to the quality of the writing and its content. Thanks must also go to Alice's father, Arvid Lundy, who got hooked into reading some of the book while visiting her. He provided an invaluable perspective as a retired scientist from Los Alamos Laboratories. Thanks also to Brenda Lightner for her amazing editorial eye. The positive responses to the material from colleagues Terry Steeden, Alison Roebuck, Mark MacWhorter, Ray Miles, and Gary Hesser also served to keep me at the task until it was finished. Some of them were among those who co-signed the original article about the Christian Right that became the basis for this book.

For the first time in my writing career, this book was a family affair. As has been the case so many times in the past, my wife, Joy, not only helped me to think through what I wanted to say, but in numerous instances she was able to bring clarity to the material I could not seem to find on my own. Her loving and patient support for my writing life is more than I deserve, but not something taken for granted. But what made this book even more special was that this time son, Jos, and daughter, Krista, got involved. They were raised on a diet of family discussions, debates, and in more than a few instances, outright arguments about religion and politics. Despite the fact that they did not always recognize the wisdom of their father's insights, I took their suggestions quite seriously. Even more, the time spent discussing the chapters is now their father's treasured moments.

I also want to say a word about the cover design. It may be that books cannot and should not be judged by their cover, but in this instance I would hope this one might be. Bob Willbanks has captured the essence of the book. The cover says it all without saying it all. Thanks also needs to go to BrownWalker Press, and Jeff Young in particular, for being open to this arrangement, and for their seeing the value of this work.

Finally, every author should have a David Polk. Before entering into quasi-retirement, David served as editor and encourager for most of my previous books. When in need, you call the person you know will help you. David responded immediately with his professional skills. More than that, he showed an excitement for what he was reading that became infectious. I actually looked forward to the next day's emails full of suggestions for improvement. Writers need someone who believes in them. For many years, and for more than a few of us, David has done his editor's work in a way that has conveyed this message. Working behind the scenes can sometimes see the value of one's labors go unrecognized. Not this time. Thus, the book's dedication.

For a decade, I have watched with growing apprehension the rise to real political influence in our country of a genuinely radical movement known as the religious right wing. This movement, whose lead organization calls itself the Christian Coalition, has a militant ideology—one that encourages deep hostility toward those who disagree with its agenda.

As a political organization, the Christian Coalition has been a great success. It is a textbook example of what a relatively small number of skilled and committed political organizers can accomplish within our democratic system. But with the Christian Coalition, I have a real problem. I consider myself a person of faith. I work very hard at being a Christian. And certainly, the Christian Coalition does not speak for me.

What's more, I am absolutely sure that the Christian Coalition does not speak for the great majority of men and women of faith in this country. And I, for one, am not prepared to stand by and permit Mr. Robertson and his friends to get away with wrapping their harsh right wing views in the banner of religious faith.

Walter Cronkite[1]

INTRODUCTION

———————————————————■———————————————————

Among a wide spectrum of religious and non-religious Americans, there is a unity of alarm, if not outrage, over the public and private assault by the Christian Right on a principle endemic to American democracy: that freedom *of* religion depends upon freedom *from* religion. Often attendant to that assault is a self-righteous and mean-spirited attitude that sees personal attacks on those who disagree with them as a legitimate method of defense for what they believe.

Concern about the Christian Right has waxed and waned since Jerry Falwell founded the now defunct Moral Majority in the late 1970s. But with the increasing degree to which the Christian Right has become a major player in the political life of the nation, the stakes have been raised considerably. What was once thought to be a fringe movement within Christianity has become the dominant Christian voice, with political clout greater than anyone imagined possible twenty-five years ago. It is not enough to shake one's head and wonder how they can say and do what they say and do, and leave it at that. This is a movement whose intentions are not to be ignored.

Who better to do that than Christians themselves? The events of 9/11 awakened the world to the dangers of religious extremism. But most American Christians still find it difficult

1

to believe Christians are capable of such extremism. The Christian Right is not a terrorist group, of course, but we believe it poses a real and present danger to the kind of free and just society that has come to be America.* At the same time, we are convinced that most American Christians do not recognize this danger. Because Christianity is the dominant religion in this country, Christians are the ones who should be leading the way in exposing the Christian Right's agenda. But that has not happened on a scale large enough to blunt their efforts. The virtual silence within the Christian community about the rise of the Christian Right is partly responsible for its gaining mainstream status. The reluctance of concerned Christians to be openly and persistently critical of the Christian Right must end. The most effective critics of Jewish and Islamic extremism are those who speak from within those traditions. The same should hold true for Christianity. The most important critics of the Christian Right must be Christians. Silence at a time such as this in the name of love is not virtuous, but shows a lack of discernment about what is happening.

Like most Americans, those of us whose views are expressed in these pages believe the events of 9/11 permanently changed the world and the role of the United States in it. The direction and meaning of the changes this catastrophic event set in motion have yet to become firmly fixed. What we can know, however, is that we must resist attempts to use 9/11 and the war on terrorism to further divide the nation along political and religious ideological lines. We believe such attempts are being made, not least by members of the Christian Right. It seems to us that they are willing to play on people's fears to advance a very narrow agenda to turn the United States into a Christian nation patterned after themselves. Those of us not aligned with them, but who identify ourselves with the Christian tradition, have a special responsibility not to sit on the sidelines and watch them use Christianity as a sword

*This book is the work of one person whose faith tradition is Christian, but it also reflects the minds and hearts of many others, Christian and non-Christian. For this reason I have chosen to use the plural pronoun "we" throughout the book, except in those few instances where personal experience added important material to the discussion.

against anyone whose views differ from theirs. We will stand with them in protecting their right to believe as they do, but we want them to know that we will also stand against them in their refusal to extend to all others the same privilege and respect.

Even though this is a book written by a Christian about Christians, we believe its message is for all Americans. We who are not hesitant to call ourselves "liberal" Christians ("open-minded") want non-Christians to know that the Christian Right does not represent what we believe, does not reflect the heart and soul of the Christianity we find in the Bible, and does not speak for us on matters of public policy. We confess that among ourselves we are not of one mind regarding the great issues of our times. But the common denominator within our ranks is the disdain we share for the Christian Right's agenda and the narrow-mindedness they display in promoting it. It is a good thing that non-Christians are uneasy about the Christian Right's influence in the political life of this nation. Christian history would suggest Christian extremism has caused much pain and suffering for them. But that is not the whole story. In every generation there have been Christians of strong faith and open minds. Without seeking to be presumptuous, we hope we stand in that tradition.

What follows, then, is an effort to expose the serious dangers the Christian Right poses to the body politic of this nation, using their own words, actions, and attitudes to indict them. Throughout the discussion, we defend liberalism in general, and liberal Christianity in particular, both of which take the brunt of their attacks. Our purpose is a simple one: to educate all Americans about a disturbing group of Christians we know well, for we occupy the same household of faith. In a sense this material consists of the content of a debate within Christian circles on which we invite non-Christians to eavesdrop. Perhaps this will help those outside our tradition to gain a better image of who Christians really are. At the least it will help them to know that, in the public arena, what they often hear as the "Christian" position hardly speaks for all who share that name. We have endeavored to speak in the spirit of peacemakers, but not without candor or passion.

1

WHEN ENOUGH BECOMES ENOUGH

In an October 6, 2002, interview on *60 Minutes*, Jerry Falwell was asked by Bob Simon, "You wrote an approving piece recently about a book called *Unveiling Islam*, And the authors of that book wrote, 'The Muslim who commits acts of violence in jihad does so with the approval of Mohammed.' Do you believe that? "

"I do," Falwell answered. "I think Mohammed was a terrorist. He—I read enough of the history of his life written by both Muslims and, and non-Muslims—that he was a, a violent man, a man of war."

"So, in the same way that Moses provided the ultimate example for the Jews and same way that Jesus provided the ultimate example for Christians, Mohammed provided the ultimate example for Muslims and he was a terrorist?" Simon responded.

"In my opinion," Falwell answered. "And I do believe that Jesus set the example for love, as did Moses. And I think that Mohammed set an opposite example."

In response to Falwell's comments, the article below appeared in the Saturday, October 19 edition of the Minneapolis *Star-Tribune*. From that point it took on a life of its own. It apparently touched a nerve among liberal Christians around the world. We hope it will continue to do so.

4

Jerry Falwell and His Christian Right Have It Wrong

Enough is enough. When Jerry Falwell declares on national television (*60 Minutes*, Oct.6, 2002) that Muhammad was a terrorist and Christians believe there will be no peace in Jerusalem until the second coming of Jesus, the time for silence on such religious arrogance is over. Put bluntly, the Christian Right Falwell represents is neither—neither Christian, nor "right."

It is not Christian in attitude and actions because both represent what Jesus spoke and acted against. The Christian Right are the Pharisees of today's Christianity. They play the role of moral and thought police who condemn to hell anyone whose actions they consider wrong and whose views are different from their own. Their religiosity runs a mile wide but their spirituality seems to be an inch deep.

The Christian Right is not right because it is intellectually dishonest. Falwell speaks as if he knows the Bible when what he actually knows is that which he already believes and imposes on the Bible. He doesn't interpret the Book of Revelation which he claims is the basis for his views on the Middle East, the fate of the world, the second coming of Jesus, and just about anything else he says he believes. Instead, he espouses the views of a man named John Darby whose interpretation of Revelation was popularized by the Scofield Bible in the nineteenth century. That's where Falwell and his Christian Right still live—in the nineteenth century when a triumphal Christianity preached a message of oppressive legalism.

The news media love to put Falwell and his kind on national television because it creates conflict. It also makes Christianity look bad. Through the years we have tried to ignore this man and others like him who are an embarrassment to many of us who claim the Christian tradition as our own. But their views have won a large following among Christians who either refuse to think for themselves or who have been duped into believing Christian Right leaders speak from understanding. They don't. Their views represent religious prejudice that draws lines in the sand that separate people into opposing camps and sows the seeds of hatred, suspicion, and war.

Those of us who are the Christians the Christian Right loves to hate have been silent for too long. In the name of tolerance we have allowed Christianity's most radical believers to turn faith into a cover for self-righteousness and love into a sword for divisiveness. It is little wonder that Christianity is in decline in America. In our view the Christian Right gives new meaning to Gandhi's comment that he might have become a Christian had he not known so many.

We confess that we have been timid to say openly that the way the Christian Right reads the Bible has at the least no credibility and at worst is patently dishonest. The moment anyone declares "The Bible says...," they are misrepresenting truth. The Bible doesn't "say" anything. Every translation is an interpretation and every preacher is an interpreter of that interpretation. So what we say the Bible says is what we have interpreted the Bible to say. To pretend otherwise is to claim knowledge not even the biblical writers claim for themselves. Even more, it ignores what any good biblical student should know, namely, that in the Bible itself there are contrasting interpretations of the ways of God, as for example the Book of Job's rejection of the Deuteronomic ethic that claims God rewards the faithful and punishes the unfaithful.

We believe the Christian Right has every right to disagree with us. They have every right to believe we are misguided in what we believe. What they do not have the right to do is to speak as if they speak for God. They do not have the right to presume that their minds are not subject to the fallibility that inflicts the rest of us. They do not have the right to claim that their views represent true Christianity and any other is condemned by God.

Americans believe all people have a right to their views. We couldn't agree more. Sadly and tragically, the Christian Right does not. That is why enough is enough![1]

Those of us who submitted the original Falwell article expected to be excoriated by the Christian Right. What we did not expect was a steady stream, at times a river, of positive responses via emails, personal letters, and telephone calls. Clearly our statement had struck a harmonious chord in more than a few Christians. Here is a sampling of the positive reactions.

> Could you hear us shouting "Amen!" from our rooftop last Saturday after reading your article? Thank you for articulating so perfectly what is in our hearts and minds. For some reason, we seem to be intimidated by the Christian right and do not often enough speak our minds. This was a wake-up call that may embolden and inspire us.

+ + +

> I have just read your editorial in the *Star Tribune*, dated October 19, and I just want to thank you and your collaborators for saying, in such a public way, what I and many of my family and friends have said over and over again. It seems like many in the media, politics, and other public realms turn to people like Falwell for the "Christian perspective," when, in fact, there is no such thing. We have a huge spectrum of ideas and opinions and beliefs within the umbrella of the Christian tradition, and I'm glad that you shared that with the public.

+ + +

> Thanks for your trenchant message regarding Jerry Falwell and his exegesis. I'm afraid his hermeneutics carry the day in the White House and Congress these days, but it's good to see that the spirit of Christ yet lives.

We did receive negative emails and letters, and more than a few phone calls. But the surprise was the overwhelming percentage of positive responses, some coming from as far away as England, Norway, and Nepal. It is clear that there is a deep and wide level of frustration with the Christian Right that needs to be voiced—that more Christians than we had realized feel disenfranchised by their own faith tradition, tolerating extremism without embracing it, but frustrated that it is the primary public voice of Christianity today. A simple statement in a public venue gave them a voice. In turn, their heartening reaction made us realize that we were not the only Christians in America who had had enough of Falwell and the Christian Right. Thus, this book was born.

2

WHO ARE THEY?

As frustrating as Falwell's public comments are, he is a lightning rod for a much larger group of radical Christians called the Christian Right. But if you believe right-wing writer Ann Coulter, the Christian Right doesn't really exist—except in the minds of liberals.

> Like all propagandists, liberals create mythical enemies to justify their own viciousness and advance their agenda. There is no bogeyman that strikes greater terror in the left than the apocryphal "religious right." The very phrase is a meaningless concept, an inverted construct of the left's own Marquis de Sade lifestyle. It functions as a talismanic utterance to rally the faithful against anyone who disagrees with the well-organized conspiratorial left.[1]

We shall have more to say about Coulter's invective writings later, but we admit that on one level what she says about the "religious right" is probably more correct than even she realizes. The "religious right" is made up of political ultra-conservatives that happen to be religious. As liberal Christians we have no quarrel with such people, although we certainly disagree with them. Religious or political conservatives are not the object of our concern. No, our quarrel is with the "Christian Right" who apparently don't know they don't exist. They believe themselves to be very real and with a very clear agenda for promoting their political views in the name of their religion and trying to legislate their religious beliefs. Pat Robertson wrote, for example:

> The Christian Coalition is launching an effort in selected states to become acquainted with the registered voters in every precinct. This is slow, hard work. But it will build a significant database to use to communicate with those people who are regular voters. When they are mobilized in support of vital issues, elected officials will listen...We must rebuild the foundation of a free, sovereign America from the grassroots, precinct by precinct, city by city, and state by state...
>
> My goal is to see a pro-freedom majority in the United States Senate in 1992, and a reversal of leadership in the House of Representatives in 1996. My associates are now publishing a newspaper called the *Christian American*, which is slated for a circulation of ten million during this decade. Since in most congressional or senatorial elections a five percent swing in the vote means victory or defeat, the power of the concept of a free, sovereign America is so strong that, if properly presented, it can sweep the one worlders out of contention in the public policy arena in a short time.[2]

This sounds like a real group of people to us, and makes us wonder why Coulter's "research" didn't uncover them for her. At any rate, if these were simply Pat Robertson groupies, as Coulter believes, with conservative political views, our concerns would be bogus. But this is not the case. The Christian Right is comprised of highly organized, well-financed groups of radicals who insist that they alone are "real" Christians. While these different Christian Right groups compete among themselves for attention, money, and power, they are united in their efforts to label liberals as unAmerican and anti-God. The arrogance of their claims is what we find offensive and dangerous.

We, therefore, beg to differ with the notion that the Christian Right is the brainchild of liberals who want to beat up on conservative Christians. They are in fact people who are well known, people of wealth, power, and influence. Indeed, members of the Christian Right are the movers and shakers in American life today. They are religious leaders such as Jerry Falwell, Pat Robertson, James Dobson, and James Kennedy. They are also political leaders such as Attorney General John Ashcroft, Senate Majority Leader Bill Frist, Assistant Majority Leader Mitch McConnell, House Majority Leader Tom DeLay, Speaker of the House Dennis Hastert, Majority Whip Roy Blunt, Oklahoma Senator James Inhofe, and Alabama leaders Bob Riley, William Pryor, and Roy Moore—the current Governor, Attorney General, and Chief Justice respectively—all of whom have been in the news for various reasons,[3] and Phyliss Schlafly, whose views are as radical as anyone among the Christian Right.[4] There are numerous others. In fact, in 2002, 178 members of the House of Representatives identified themselves with the Christian Right.[5]

The most prominent Christian Right politician in America today is President George Bush. An acknowledged "born again" Christian, Mr. Bush does not demonstrate the kind of venomous spirit in attacking liberal Christians that is ubiquitous among other Christian Right leaders. Nevertheless, his policies and public statements support the Christian Right's agenda about the kind of government we should have and what role America should play in world affairs. For example, Mr. Bush wants tax dollars used to support faith-based initiatives among Christian groups that discriminate against people who do not share their religious or moral views. When given the opportunity he has nominated and appointed people to the federal bench who are openly members of the Christian Right. These names come to mind: William Pryor, previously mentioned, who once wrote, "God has chosen through his son, Jesus Christ, this time and this place for all Christians...to save our country and save our courts;"[6] James Leon Holmes, former president of the Arkansas Right to Life, who said, "the wife is to subordinate herself to her husband;"[7] and Priscilla Owen, the Texas justice who once told a teenage minor she needed to prove she understood religious objections to abortion.[8]

What the Christian Right has come to realize is that politicians come and go, but justices are forever. If you want to change the nature of the American experience, you get justices appointed at every level. Mr. Bush seems quite willing to do all he can to enact this portion of the agenda for reshaping America into their image.

Perhaps even more revealing, Mr. Bush has made public statements that leave little doubt about how he views his own job and the role America must play in the world. In a conversation with Palestinian Prime Minister Mahmound Abbas, he said,

> God told me to strike at Al-Qaida and I struck them, and then he instructed me to strike at Saddam, which I did, and now I am determined to solve the problem in the Middle East. If you help me, I will act, and if not, the elections will come and I will have to focus on them.[9]

We see nothing wrong with Mr. Bush or any other political leader claiming to be a "born again" Christian, though we do admit it makes us very nervous when he claims his actions are based on God telling him what to do. Most troubling, however, is the fact that the Christian Right claims him as one of their own, and he seems to welcome it. In his book, *Persecution: How Liberals Are Waging War Against Christianity*, about which we will have much more to say later, David Limbaugh characterizes criticism of Bush and his policies as an attack on Bush's attempt to put his faith in action. In an extended section defending him, Limbaugh concludes,

> Christians cannot and should not build a firewall between their private lives and their public persona, between their Christianity and their governance. It is impossible for anyone, including the president, to separate his belief system, his worldview, from his public life."[10]

His statement suggests that Mr. Bush is simply living out his faith. That is too simplistic. When the most powerful man in the world says he is being led by God to do what he does, it is much more than saying he is trying to live his faith. He is implying that to disagree with his decisions is to disagree with God. Moreover, what Limbaugh and the Christian Right ignore is the fact that Muslim terrorists whom they believe are the epitome of evil also claim to be serving God. Excessive radicalism can cut many ways. That one is a Christian does not justify political policies. Fundamentalist theology exists in Judaism and Islam as well as Christianity.

This is not to say that all fundamentalists are members of the Christian Right. Many are not. Moreover, some of them, especially within academic institutions, have views that reflect both humility and open-mindedness,[11] neither of which the Christian Right can be accused of demonstrating. More to the point, what distinguishes the Christian Right from other Christian fundamentalists is that its members *immerse their ultra-conservative political views and agenda in Christian baptism.* They do not hesitate labeling anyone who disagrees with them as immoral and anti-Christian. This is done openly and in subtle ways, and is present in and through all their words and actions. It, in fact, drives them. They thrive on having an enemy who must be vanquished.

This is what sets the Christian Right apart. Political activism by Christians is not a new or bad thing. What makes the Christian Right who they are is their exclusive claim to being Christian and following Christian morality. In making this claim they also demonize anyone whose views challenge theirs. In their world disagreement makes for enemies. Liberals are particularly that enemy. They are the people the Christian Right loves to hate. And that is not too strong a word to use when talking about the Christian Right. They speak of "hating the sin but loving the sinner," but fail miserably in their effort, if in fact they make any effort at all. They believe they are right because they are Christian and, therefore, have a corner on truth that is available to no one else. They hide their prejudice and close-mindedness behind a thin veil of religious slogans and Bible quotes that tell everything about them but nothing about the truth they claim to be espousing.

It's not that those who disagree with the Christian Right are always right on issues. What distinguishes us is that we do not believe God is on *our* side in our disagreements, or that *we alone* know the mind of God when it comes to complex issues. We do not call our opponents "godless" conservatives. We do not believe God is going to send them to "hell." We are willing, instead, to keep the debate on a human level and leave God out of it. We think that over the centuries Christians have done enough damage naming the enemies of God without our adding to it.

The Christian Right, of course, will have none of this. They are determined to drag God and the Bible into every comment they make about their enemies. We believe they are doing great damage to the nation and to Christianity. Non-Christians do not make the kinds of distinctions between Christians that we make among ourselves. Instead, they judge us by our public face, much the way Christians draw conclusions about other faith traditions. It distresses us that what non-Christians think of all Christians is in large part determined by what they hear from Christianity's loudest voice today, the Christian Right. But even more sobering is the danger the Christian Right poses to the enduring principles of this nation. They are convinced this is a Christian nation and are, therefore, working hard to transform our present form of government into a Christian state. We will show that to achieve this goal they have adopted an ethic of "ends justifying means." It is very troubling that a group of people who claim to be the only genuine Christians, and also the only true people of God, act this way. At the very least it requires those of us who claim to be of the same faith tradition to challenge what the Christian Right stands for and what it seeks to do.

Given who they are, it is little wonder they scare non-Christians. Truth be told, they scare other Christians! But not enough to keep us quiet.

3

WHO ARE WE?

And so, who are "we" who would call ourselves liberal Christians? Actually we come very close to fitting Ann Coulter's "apocryphal" religious group category. We are not organized. We are not well known. We do not occupy seats of major influence in a nation that lives by wealth and power, even in church circles. Worst of all, we have no money. But she says we *do* exist and she knows what we're up to.

> Liberal dogma instructs that public displays of religion are inimical to democracy, a threat to freedom as we know it. They believe religious people are self-evidently fanatical. Religious values are hateful, homophobic, sexist, racist, and the rest of the liberal catechism—unless they are kept in the closet.[1]

Coulter also presumes to know the difference between us and the Christian Right.

> The fundamental difference between liberals and conservatives is: Conservatives believe man was created in God's image; liberals believe they are God. All their other behavioral tics proceed from this irreducible minimum.[2]

She is not alone in her view about who we are and what we are up to. Based on what Gil Alexander-Moegerle, former co-founder of James Dobson's Focus on the Family, the wealthiest Christian Right group in America,[3] says, Dobson would agree with Coulter:

> According to him [Dobson], there exists a large and powerful association of liberals united in their position on various social issues of the day and who are funded in such massive proportions that they can do whatever they please, whenever they please: hire staff, distribute mass mailings, purchase print and electronic ads, lobby Congress, and "buy" legislators with campaign contributions. Their pockets give new definition to the word "deep." Furthermore, this corrupt cabal is united in the evil that permeates their hearts and motivates their actions. These are bad people who just don't care—about America, about children, about families, about God.[4]

If Dobson were right about the money and power of liberals in general, and we do not know if he is, he is certainly wrong about those of us who might rightly be called "liberal" Christians. Rather than being people of wealth and power, in general we are ordinary women and men who have grown weary of the Christian Right being the dominant religious voice in American politics. We are not radicals. We do not represent theological extremism. We have no formal organization. We do not believe we are God or that God is on our side, or anyone else's.

When it comes to politics, some of us are Republicans. Some of us are Democrats. Some of us are Independents. It is an educated guess to say that we represent what can be called a diverse but mainstream American citizenry. The one thing we share in common, the one thing that makes us liberals and Christians, is that we believe it is both possible and effective to be people who balance a strong faith with an open mind.

People of faith with open minds: That is who we are. It is what we mean when we use the label "liberal" to describe our faith stance. It refers more to a mindset than to a set of beliefs.

As such it is not unthinkable that some conservatives could be called "liberal." Liberals may disagree with one another on matters of faith or politics precisely because we are open-minded and reject the idea that anyone knows Truth without the errors of perception endemic to being human. This means we have a basic respect for interpretive differences that exist among us. Our unity lies in the value and power we see in diversity. We are not threatened by differences. Rather, we consider them the means by which we guard against the kind of extremism we see in the Christian Right.

You might think no one, especially someone of faith, would dare to wear the label "liberal" at a time when being conservative seems for many people to be a religion in itself. Yet we do. Proudly, in fact. Not that being liberal is the point. But if being "liberal" puts us in the category of listening to other points of view to a fault, then count us in. If it means we don't believe Christians have a corner on truth, and certainly not on goodness, then count us in. If it means we believe God is bigger than anything we believe about God because human beings cannot fully, and certainly not infallibly, comprehend the ways and will of God, then count us in. If it means believing the Christian Right has given Christianity a bad name, then count us in. If it means believing an open mind and a humble spirit represent the mind and heart of Christianity more than the narrow-minded, judgmentalism of the Christian Right, then count us in.

Actually, Anne Coulter is more correct about us than she probably knows, given her proclivity for exaggeration and distortion. But her assessment of our agenda needs some tweaking. For example, public religious displays are not an issue. *Christian* displays on *government property* are. Since taxes are collected from non-Christians, and since nothing in the Constitution says our government is Christian, we think such displays are in poor taste and do not respect the numerous court rulings holding them in violation of the Constitution. Of course, during holy seasons such as Christmas and Easter you can find religious displays in thousands of churchyards around the country, but apparently this is not the *freedom* Coulter and the Christian Right appreciate.

It is also true that as liberals we believe religious values are hateful, homophobic, sexist, and racist—*sometimes*! Didn't Coulter grow up in America? Doesn't she live here now? Does she actually believe churches didn't support segregation in the South in the name of racial purity, and that many churches still will not consider minorities for leadership positions? Does she actually believe criticizing restrictions on the civil liberties of homosexuals who pay taxes just as she does is an example of liberals trying to tear down America?

We are guilty as charged when she suggests we believe religious values are hateful. We don't believe this has to be the case, or that it is all the time. But much of the hatred the world has known and knows today has been and is rooted in religion. As one liberal Christian puts it:

> Religion is arguably the most powerful and pervasive force on earth. Throughout history religious ideas and commitments have inspired individuals and communities of faith to transcend narrow self-interests in pursuit of higher values and truths. The record of history shows that noble acts of love, self-sacrifice, and service to others are frequently rooted in deeply religious worldviews. At the same time, history clearly shows that religion has often been linked directly to the worst examples of human behavior. It is somewhat trite, but nevertheless sadly true, to say that more wars have been waged, more people killed, and these days more evil perpetrated in the name of religion than by any other institutional force in history.[5]

Though the above perspective does not apply solely to Christianity, as liberal Christians we believe it does indict our faith tradition. This admission does not mean we want to tear down the faith that gives our lives meaning and purpose. It means we believe telling the truth about ourselves is core to public credibility.

According to the Christian Right, however, being liberal means we are either not real Christians, or not loyal Americans, or both. They seem to think that being open minded means compromising one's personal integrity. The message we hear in their criticisms is that liberals won't tell people how to think, and liberal Christians won't tell people what God wants them to believe! Reading between the lines of their criticisms, it seems they consider an open mind to be a dangerous thing, the tool of the Devil, and evidence that liberalism represents an assault on the truth of God.

We take these criticisms seriously, and plead guilty as charged. We do believe that it is rare indeed when one person can tell another what God thinks about any controversial issue. We subscribe to the notion that the human mind is always subject to faulty thinking. This is why we believe the most reliable truth is that which comes from within a community of dialogue where points of view are subjected to constant critical review. We believe no one has a corner on truth, that no mind is capable of perfect perception, and that no one, especially a Christian, should dare speak as if he or she has special access to the mind or the heart of God.

Who are we? We are Christians who are blessed with the joy of being able to disagree with each other without rancor or making charges of heresy. We are Christians whose faith thrives on challenge and debate and study and all the rest that goes with serious thinking. We are Christians who have tired of the continuing public embarrassment cast on Christianity by the likes of Jerry Falwell and Pat Robertson. We are Christians who are not afraid to say that if the Christianity of the Christian Right were the only alternative, we would choose not to be Christian. The good news, though, is that we know it isn't, and have decided to say so publicly. So when members of the Christian Right criticize us for being "liberal," we count it as a compliment. It means we disagree with their view of the world, and that is one "truth" on which we all can agree.

4

ENOUGH OF BIBLICAL ABUSE

∎

The Christian Right claims to follow the Bible. This is the basis for phrases like "the Christian position" or "biblical values" or "Christian morality." They see themselves as those who have been given the responsibility to be the true voice of God today. They contend the rest of us are imposters or, even worse, agents of Satan who is using us to battle the forces of good.

As liberal Christians we want to challenge the Christian Right precisely where they claim to speak with authority: the way they read the Bible. First and foremost, we challenge the claim that all they do is believe the Bible. It is an appealing phrase, but hides truth rather than revealing it. To say you believe the Bible means that you believe your understanding of the Bible. Nothing wrong with that. That's what we all do. Unfortunately the Christian Right doesn't want to admit it. We do. They choose, instead, to claim they believe what the Bible says and that liberals interpret and twist what the Bible says because deep down we just don't believe it. Christian Right preachers, therefore, don't hesitate to say, "The Bible says…" Liberals, on the other hand, add an essential phrase, "as far as I understand it." There is good reason for saying this.

It shouldn't be news to Christians, but the Bible was not written in English. Not even in German, French, Italian, or Russian. Not only did Jesus not speak any of these languages, we don't know if he spoke Hebrew or Greek, the two languages of the original Bible. So far as we can determine, he spoke a Hebrew dialect called Aramaic. It is possible that he spoke Hebrew. Being born in a culture where Greek was the dominant language, it is also possible that he spoke Greek. But most Bible scholars, including conservatives, believe his native tongue was Aramaic. That means that the biblical writers themselves had to translate his words. Then once the Bible had been compiled it was translated into Latin, which, of course, only priests could read. The combination of the invention of the printing press and, later, the Protestant Reformation, resulted in a flood of translations into modern languages. When Christian Right preachers say they are preaching the Bible, they are in fact preaching an English translation of the "Bible." Perhaps some of them read Hebrew and Greek. That would make them less dependent on an English translation and put them closer to the original texts, except that we don't have any! No original manuscript exists. So the truth is, when Christian Right preachers declare, "The Bible says..." as if they possess the very words of the biblical authors, it isn't true. They are preaching a translation of copies of the original books, and then only fragments that are pieced together.

The problem, of course, is actually even more complicated. Not only is their Bible a translation of manuscript copies, when they begin telling someone else what it says rather than letting them read for themselves, they automatically and inescapably start interpreting the Bible. Herein lies an example of a slick trick of the trade Christian Right preachers have perfected. They have convinced their followers that when they speak, the Bible speaks, and when they are silent, the Bible is silent. In effect what this means is that people abdicate their own common sense in order to accept what their leaders are saying. It is a pervasive problem in this country.

In his book, *The Death of Common Sense*, attorney Phillip Howard argues that too many Americans have given up their God-given power to think for themselves.[1] He may not have been thinking about the followers of Christian Right preachers, but he was certainly describing their behavior. These people are willing to believe what on its face is ridiculous. Perhaps this illustration will help.

Imagine that you and a Christian Right preacher see the same accident. Afterwards he tells you that it doesn't matter what you may have seen. What really happened is what he says happened. Therefore you must believe what he says and you will be safe. The moment you do you abandon your own common sense that is screaming inside your head that you are crazy to believe what he saw is the only version of the accident.

This is how the Christian Right read and preach the Bible and how they expect their followers to respond. If the Bible says homosexuality is an abomination before God (Leviticus 20:13), then it is. No interpretation is involved. Never mind the fact that the same book—Leviticus—says that disobedient children and adulterers should be executed (Leviticus 20:9–10). Never mind the fact that the Christian Right says these commands don't apply to today's world. No interpretation is involved in that either. People who believe this are captive Christians, captive to a narrow-minded, authoritarian mindset that passes itself off as God's mind, justifying itself by refusing to be honest in discussing the reasons for its point of view, captives to throwing their common sense out the window.

Liberal Christians know that anyone who tells another person what the Bible says is an interpreter of the Bible. We think this is a good thing. We have no fear of interpretation because we trust that in a community of faith where people are free to discuss various points of view, the Word of God is heard without fear or coercion. This is how the books in the Bible got there in the first place. They do not speak the Word of God because they are in the Bible. They are in the Bible because Christians heard the Word of God in them. But to hear the Christian Right talk, you would think the Bible fell out of heaven and landed in their hands.

The motivation behind this kind of errant reasoning is transparent, of course. It's authority. Not the Bible's authority. Theirs. This is the primary leverage Christian Right leaders use to promote their political agenda. To come clean to their people about the Bible would weaken their position of authority. They would be seen as giving an interpretation of God's Word rather than the very Word of God itself. Presenting their views as God's Word takes every debate to a very different level where opponents can be cast as people opposed to God's truth. It is a clever move, dishonest as it may be. And it has proven to be effective in putting liberal Christians in the position of defending the genuineness of their faith.

Another tool the Christian Right uses to augment their authority is fear. They speak freely and often about God's judgment being ever ready to strike, and to strike down. That is why Falwell said that planes flying into the Twin Towers and the Pentagon were the result of the judgment of God, just as he said years before that God's hand was in a plane crash near Chicago that killed *Playboy* executives. What is curious about the Christian Right's insider's knowledge of divine retribution is that they always seem to be exempt from it. Everyone else should beware of the hammer of the Lord, but not them. It seems their secret knowledge of the ways of God includes knowing what side of the judgment line they stand on.

Hell, of course, is the big dread the Christian Right exploits. They push the envelope when it comes to holding people over the abyss. After all, nobody likes being told they're going to hell. It doesn't matter that the existence of a "place" called hell is to mislead people into thinking of it in time and space categories. Eternity, "hell," or "heaven" are not time and space concepts. The only language that can speak of the mystery they represent is the language of existence. God exists in the sense that God "is." The great "I am" does not reside in a place called "heaven." It's metaphorical language, the language of poetry, used to describe what is beyond description and beyond experience. But the Christian Right literalizes it. They turn metaphorical language the Bible uses to describes a state of "estrangement" from God into time and space language that makes "hell" an actual place.

From here they intensify the language of fear with "the end is near" theology. Rather than understanding the book of Revelation as material written for first-century Christians as a source of encouragement against doubt and persecution, they turn it into a calendar of future events that are always about to happen. Further, they interject into "the end is near" thinking what they call "the rapture." According to the Christian Right, "the rapture" is what the apostle Paul was talking about in 1 Thessalonians 4:17 when he wrote: "Then we who are alive, who are left, will be caught up in the clouds together with them to meet the Lord in the air; and so we will be with the Lord forever." Christians (read, "the Christian Right") will be taken up to heaven before the tribulation (punishment) of sinners who have been "left behind" begins.

This, we believe, is a misunderstanding of this text popularized by a nineteenth-century preacher named John Darby, whose views were incorporated into the popular Scofield Bible. As orthodox British theologian N. T. Wright has said of turning Paul's words into "the rapture":

> Paul's description of Jesus' reappearance in 1 Thessalonians 4 is a brightly colored version of what he says in two other passages, 1 Corinthians 15:51–54 and Philippians 3:20–21: At Jesus' "coming" or "appearing," those who are still alive will be "changed" or "transformed" so that their mortal bodies will become incorruptible, deathless. This is all that Paul intends to say in Thessalonians, but here he borrows imagery—from biblical and political sources—to enhance his message. Little did he know how his rich metaphors would be misunderstood two millennia later.[2]

Obviously people respond to "scare theology." The *Left Behind* series of books co-authored by Tim LaHaye, who helped Falwell found the Moral Majority, have sold millions.[3] If you've ever been in a "Christian" bookstore the day one of the books was released, you've seen the mad rush to get one each installment creates. Stacks of them go like hot cakes. That, however, does not change the fact that they misuse the Bible by offering their interpretations of "truth" as truth itself. We admit that in the battle over the Bible, we hardly gave them a fight. Maybe that's because we didn't think it was all that important to modern-minded Christians in the first place. We were wrong. It matters a lot. Christians may not know the Bible, an indisputable fact these days, but, ironically, they claim to believe what it says. Since liberal Christians essentially "gave" the Bible away, what most people believe is either what the

Christian Right is telling them it says or an amalgamation of biblical phrases they have heard over the years and pieced together into their own authorized version. Either way, through neglect, liberal Christianity gave up our seat at the discussion table and walked away.

We want back in. The Christian Right doesn't own the Bible anymore than they own Jesus or God. Their beliefs are not only misguided, but in many instances amount to spiritual abuse in the way many Christian Right preachers exploit fear to their own end. We find their ways unconscionable. Few on our side of this battle have been willing to criticize their tactics in an open and frank manner. We have decided it is time to do so. Too much is at stake to pretend that it is acceptable to read the Bible any way you want as long as you're sincere. That has led to too much suffering already. Christians need to call the hand of Christians abusing their position by claiming an authority reserved only for God. God is not limited or explained fully by what the Christian Right claim the Bible says. Both Jews and Christians existed as communities of faith hundreds of years before either had any written authority they called "scripture." To believe the Bible speaks the Word of God to all generations is not the same thing as one group of Christians saying that what they believe *is* the Word of God.

Even more important is the fact that the Bible doesn't need the protection the Christian Right wants to provide. The power of its truth is sufficient to win the hearts and minds of people without the use of fear or coercion. The Christian Right's use of both creates an image of God that leads one to conclude that human beings make better parents than God. What kind of parents want their children to love them because the children fear being punished if they don't. This is not the image of God we believe Jesus talked about. A waiting Father who receives a wayward son back, or loves another in spite of his inability to forgive his brother, is not a punishing God. An owner of a vineyard who is free to be gracious to workers who came late is not a punishing God. A teacher who tells an adulterous woman that she is not condemned even though a religious law says otherwise is not a punishing God. So the God we hear the Christian Right talking about is one we do not and cannot believe in.

Yet, the entire political agenda of the Christian Right rests on this negative image of a God who will some day exact a pound of flesh from anyone who turns from the straight and narrow path, a path the Christian Right has defined to suit its own needs. It is not surprising, although quite disconcerting, that Falwell believes the ACLU and other organizations "have attempted to secularize America, have removed our nation from its relationship with Christ on which it was founded." So why wouldn't he conclude, "I therefore believe that they created an environment which possibly has caused God to lift the veil of protection which has allowed no one to attack America on our soil since 1812."[4]

Pat Robertson responded to Falwell's statement with a prayer:

> We have sinned against Almighty God, at the highest level of our government, we've stuck our finger in your eye. The Supreme Court has insulted you over and over again, Lord. They've taken your Bible away from the schools. They've forbidden little children to pray. They've taken the knowledge of God as best they can, and organizations have come into court to take the knowledge of God out of the public square of America.[5]

What is astonishing is that people believe the Christian Right. After centuries of being warned the end of the world is near and divine punishment awaits all non-Christians, people still give credibility to this kind of self-serving, judgmental theology. Even more astonishing is that there are some Zionist Jews who believe the Christian Right is a friend to Israel. I remember when former Israeli Prime Minister Menachem Begin came to Falwell's campus to thank him for his support of Israel. Apparently it didn't matter to Begin that Falwell's support of the state of Israel stems primarily from his belief that the return of the Jews to their ancient homeland will set the stage for the Second Coming of Christ, which will include salvation for all Jews who convert and condemnation for those who do not.

Ed McAteer, a former Colgate marketing executive who joined Falwell in founding the Moral Majority, declared, "The Bible does not contain the word of God. Listen to me closely.

The Bible *is* the word of God." He went on to say, "I believe that we are seeing prophecy unfold so rapidly and dramatically and wonderfully and, without exaggerating, makes me breathless."[6]

What leaves the Christian Right "breathless" is the expansion of Israeli settlements on the West Bank which they see as another sign of the coming end. According to their view, the land belongs to the Jews; Palestinians are intruders on the plans of God. Thus, McAteer claims, "Every grain of sand, every grain of sand between the Dead Sea, the Jordan River, and the Mediterranean Sea belongs to the Jews."[7] He goes further and declares that the bulk of Palestinians need to be moved to some Arab country because nothing can come between the Jews and their land.[8]

Some members of the Christian Right are convinced God intends all of Palestine to belong to Israel. They even suggest God was behind the assassination of Prime Minister Yitzchak Rabin who signed the Oslo Accord between Israel and the Palestinians, that includes Israel's relinquishment of the West Bank. The views of Kay Arthur, who heads an organization called Precept Ministries based in Chattanooga, represents how radical the Christian Right can be on this subject: "They were going against the word of God. You cannot go against the word of God. And I believe that God stopped it. I think that God did not want that Oslo Accord to go through."[9]

Such support for Israel is not something to write home about, however. Arthur also says, "The Jews need conversion. They need to know that the Messiah is coming. And the Bible tells us what's going to happen."[10] As arrogant as that attitude is, it gets worse. The Christian Right actually believes there will be a personification of the anti-Christ concept found in the book of *Revelation* and that such a person will in fact be Jewish.[11]

Jewish leaders without a Zionist political agenda see through this charade.[12] Gershom Gorenberg, author of *The End of Days*, a book critical of Christians who support Israel because of their literal reading of the Bible, says,

> The Jews die or convert. As a Jew, I can't feel very comfortable with the affections of somebody who looks

forward to that scenario. They don't love real Jewish people. They love us as characters in their story, in their play, and that's not who we are, and we never auditioned for that part, and the play is not one that ends up good for us. If you listen to the drama they're describing, essentially it's a five-act play in which the Jews disappear in the fourth act.[13]

Yossi Alpher, who served twelve years in Israel's intelligence agency, the Mossad, and later became Director of the American Jewish Committee, agrees with Gorenberg. "God save us from these people," he says. "When you see what these people are encouraging Israel and the U.S. Administration to do, that is, ignore the Palestinians, if not worse, if not kick them out, expand the settlements to the greatest extent possible, they are leading us into a scenario of out-and-out disaster."[14]

Liberal Christians share the above sentiments. With friends like the Christian Right, Israel doesn't need enemies. The theology their reading of the Bible represents is an extremist worldview that is neither biblically justifiable nor politically realistic. The beliefs of the Christian Right in regard to the Middle East are incendiary. This does not make them unchristian or anti-God, as they would say of us. But it does mean that even as faithful Muslims reject terrorist claims that they are following the Qu'ran, so we reject the Christian Right's claim that it is following biblical teaching. What they are doing is following *their* understanding of the Bible. Moreover, we do not subscribe to the notion all interpretations are equal. Being entitled to one's opinion does not preclude the fact that one can be off base. Opinions do not carry equal credibility. Christians sitting on a hillside waiting for the world to end during the Y2K hysteria were entitled to do so, but sensible people did not have put any trust in their predictions.

It is time for liberal Christians to be bolder in our criticism of the Christian Right and the way they twist the Bible to suit their political aims. The way they read the Bible is not the way we read it. The God they believe in is not the God we believe in. The Jesus they follow is not the Jesus we find in the New Testament gospels. We realize that the differences between us are based on the way each of us interprets the Bible. We say this openly. Their claims would have more credibility if they did as well.

5

Enough of Christianizing America

The Christian Right sees itself engaged in a battle between good and evil to save America. Below, for example, are the views of the founding members of the Alliance Defense Fund (ADF), a Christian Right legal group, as posted on its web site.[1]

Bill Bright (Campus Crusade for Christ): "I truly believe we are fighting for the very survival of the Gospel and of evangelism in America today."

Larry Burkett (Crown Financial Ministries): "The legal attacks on our religious freedom are escalating at an alarming rate. Through ADF, we can unite, pool resources, and help defend our rights."

James Dobson (Focus on the Family): "I urge every Christian to stand with me in support of ADF's critical case-funding work. Already, ADF is having a powerful impact in the nation's courts."

D. James Kennedy (Coral Ridge Ministries): "Through ADF's crucial work, we have a fighting chance to preserve America's true heritage and value system. Please pray and support ADF's efforts."

Marlin Maddoux ("Point of View" Radio Program): "ADF gives Christians a unique way to fight back against the radical attacks of groups like the ACLU, homosexual activists, and anti-family activists."[2]

These statements reflect the attitude within the Christian Right that its agenda is what God wants for America. One of the most passionate voices among them for this agenda is D. James Kennedy, minister at Coral Ridge Presbyterian Church in Fort Lauderdale, Florida and founder of Coral Ridge Ministries. On the web site of his Center for Reclaiming America, he makes an appeal that is forthright in its goals.

> Words are no longer enough. Not any more. America has already experienced too steep and profound a moral decline. It is time for action on the local grassroots level.
>
> This is why we need you as a volunteer with the CENTER FOR RECLAIMING AMERICA. God has given us an incredibly gifted staff for the CENTER—but they can only accomplish a small portion of our vision. The rest is up to concerned believers like you. Please respond today to let us know that God is calling you to help!
>
> This is a challenge we must meet—for the sake of our beloved country...for the sake of our beloved children and grandchildren, who will inherit the nation we leave behind...and for the cause of Christ, which has suffered such oppression at the hands of the anti-virtue radicals over recent decades.
>
> Please join me in a truly effective effort to reclaim our nation for Christ![3]

Years ago Kennedy preached a sermon on his weekly television show in which he captivated his Sunday morning audience with a recitation of Patrick Henry's "Give Me Liberty, Or Give Me Death" speech delivered at St. John's Church in Richmond, Virginia in 1775. Though Henry's speech was and is one of the great pieces of oratory born of the American fight for independence, it was not in any sense a speech about Christianity. Ignoring both the content and historical context, Kennedy used it to support his efforts to Christianize America.

For the Christian Right, reference to God in early American documents translates "Christian."

One of the ways the Christian Right promotes this determination to Christianize America is to hold Fourth of July celebrations as if it were a Christian holiday. Jerry Falwell's Liberty University and *The Old Time Gospel Hour* join together in hosting prominent Christian Right politicians whose speeches are laced with "Christian America" language. As Falwell himself has said, "The idea that religion and politics don't mix was invented by the Devil to keep Christians from running their own country."[4] But he is not talking about religion and politics. He's talking about *Christianity* and politics. Nor is it even politics. It is government-sponsored religion. Thus, he argues,

> There is no separation of church and state. Modern U.S. Supreme Courts have raped the Constitution and raped the Christian faith and raped the churches by misinterpreting what the Founders had in mind in the First Amendment to the Constitution.[5]

Thus, he goes on to say,

> If we are going to save America and evangelize the world, we cannot accommodate secular philosophies that are diametrically opposed to Christian truth. We need to pull out all the stops to recruit and train 25 million Americans to become informed pro-moral activists whose voices can be heard in the halls of Congress. I am convinced that America can be turned around if we will all get serious about the Master's business. It may be late, but it is never too late to do what is right. We need an old-fashioned, God-honoring, Christ-exalting revival to turn American back to God. America can be saved![6]

What Falwell is saying is vintage thinking among the Christian Right. It is why Christian Right churches hold "I love America" worship services without the slightest discomfort. The fact that the First Amendment is intentionally religiously neutral even as it accommodates the free exercise of religion does not factor into their thinking. They seldom allow facts to get in the way of their opinions. As one web site claims,

> Here in America the persecution of Christians has not reached the feverish pitch as it has in other parts of the world. There is a Constitution that still protects them and allows them to freely practice their faith. But boiling beneath the surface, the same hatred for God that exists in all other parts of the world is festering in all our institutions. Slowly, methodically, and incrementally the anti-God forces are working to remove that barrier. In America it is called "secularism" and is becoming visible in all walks of life and in all our institutions. Numerous legislative and legal battles which I will discuss later attest to the fact that religious warfare is taking place.

The author of the above statement goes on to say he believes Christians in this nation are being subjected to discrimination, recrimination, and stand in danger of outright persecution.

> There is an assault going on—and the liberal social engineers have declared that Christians are the enemy. Amidst their cries of "diversity" and "tolerance" it has become fashionable to bash Christians, discriminate against them, and to deny the Christian roots of American democracy.
>
> They resent how Christians pose constant reminders to them—and to an American society that is unsure about following them—that God has absolute standards of right and wrong.
>
> These anti-Christian liberals want to achieve a new, humanistic America where our children will be protected from outmoded Christian ideas and will enjoy freedom **"from"** religion—not freedom "of" religion. They do not respect God's definition of the family and are intent on discrediting His wisdom in raising children as they attempt to rewrite His guidelines for morality.
>
> These social liberals believe man has the only answers for himself. They think that perhaps a new,

man-made spirituality eventually may be useful in managing the populace—but frankly would prefer that it not be a moralistic religion with rules or absolute right and wrong. They certainly do not want the new society they are molding to hang onto any "biased" religion that proclaims Jesus Christ is the Only Way (John 14:6) or that all men and women are called by their Creator to have a warm, personal relationship with Him. We Christians irritate these social liberals when we proclaim the truth of God's liberating love. We infuriate them when we remind them of our Lord's true and steadfast faithfulness.[7]

With 80 to 85 percent of the American public claiming to be Christian, and assuming that this writer does not believe the Christian Right would persecute themselves, we can guess who the guilty party is. It is anyone who disagrees with him. And in point of fact, this is absolutely true. We have no desire or need to persecute the Christian Right, but we are eager to criticize them for being more American than Christian in their loyalties. We believe they believe devotion to country is loyalty to God. Their mantra is, "My country: Love it or leave it." American "might" makes America "right" because Americans are God's new chosen people.

What all of this means is that the business of the Christian Right is to re-christianize America. This is the goal of their political agenda. The 2003 Texas legislature is a case in point. Emboldened by their election sweep in 2002, the Republican majority decided to enact what they openly called a Christian Right agenda into Texas law. One proposal gave the Christian Right members of the state board of education control over school textbooks. Another reinstated school prayer. All the while these same lawmakers were working to remove 250,000 poor children from the Children's Health Insurance Program. We fail to see what is "Christian" about such actions.

But the point is that the extremism in the Texas legislature reveals how radical the agenda of the Christian Right is. Their pet issue of prayer in public schools provides a rallying point for a host of social legislation they are working to enact. The first five chapters of David Limbaugh's book mentioned earlier consist of a litany of all the ways liberals are waging war on Christianity. Banning prayer in schools, refusing to allow Christian students to witness to their faith, using curriculum that is anti-Christian, are some of the assaults on Christianity he mentions. But the agenda leaves little doubt that the Christian Right doesn't want equal treatment in the public arena. Its goal is dominance, believing that Christianity is the foundation upon which America was built. Thus, they don't want prayer in schools. They want *Christian* prayers in schools. They want prayer that expresses their beliefs that America is a Christian nation. Anyone who disagrees is anti-Christian and betrays the intentions of the nation's founders.

We believe their agenda is dangerous. We reject the notion that the founders intended this nation to have a Christian government. We read the Constitution as establishing a religiously neutral nation. As much as we abhor the secularization of the nation's values, we stand with those liberal voices—religious and non-religious—that argue that the only recourse we have to change the situation is dialogue rather than coercion via legislation.

Here is where we—as American liberal Christians—find ourselves in direct conflict with the Christian Right. They want the government to be an instrument of Christianity. We do not. They believe the intention of the separation of church and state was to prevent the state from intruding into church matters. We agree *and* also believe, as did Thomas Jefferson, that it was intended to prevent the church from intruding into state matters.[8] There is ample opportunity for religion to influence American politics through individuals, but we oppose the Christian Right's efforts to impose their views on the nation through legislation without respect for religious diversity.

At the moment we are losing the battle, not only with the electorate, but in regard to the avenue of choice that has become the Christian Right's major battleground, the American judicial system. The strength of the Christian Right's political influence suggests they are in a position to make impressive gains in Christian Right judges being nominated and confirmed at both federal and state levels. We consider this to be part of an effort to create an informal theocratic state with their views of Christian morality as the final arbiter. They clearly believe that a Christian nation should be led by their kind of Christians. The Christian Right wants a Christian America not unlike the theocratic state of Iran. They, of course, object to this characterization, but they do not explain why it does not apply. Theocracies differ only in terms of the religious tradition. Extremism under any religious banner is still extremism.

The Christian Right does not want to be cast in this light because they know that Americans distrust Muslim theocracies. But they cannot avoid it. They argue that secular liberalism is a "religion" in its own right and does not represent America's "Christian origins" to which they want to return. They apparently believe that the issue of church and state is not one of separation, but turns on which "religion" determines government policy. They do not seek formal ties between church and state, but they do want the state to reflect their beliefs and values and worldview to the extent that any separation between the two would be meaningless. Thus, in subtle and not so subtle ways, they are working to make America a reflection of themselves.

In this regard, we would argue that they are less faithful to the faith they proclaim than those of us who do not share their views. As American Christians, our loyalty lies first with the teachings of Jesus Christ, somewhat of an irony, given the Christian Right's rejection of what we believe. Our faith is what informs our patriotism and shapes our response to government policies and actions. We believe in capitalism, but refuse to ignore the fact that, when unregulated, it often works to reward those who have much and penalizes those who have little. We believe in people picking themselves up by their own bootstraps, but will not ignore those who have no boots. We grieved the loss of life that occurred on September 11, 2001 as much as anyone, but are not willing to be silent when justice becomes selective in the name of national security.

It seems to us that the Christian Right has lost perspective when it comes to church and state, Christianity and patriotism. We don't take for granted the freedom and opportunities we enjoy as American Christians, but neither do we believe patriotism requires denying or ignoring injustices and inequities our nation tolerates and even perpetuates. We are deeply disturbed that the Christian Right is so nationalistic in its condemnation of "evil" that it seems to ignore the fact that our government also supports unjust and unethical policies and behavior.[9] Equating patriotism with uncritical support of government policies is not democracy. Rather, democracy means having a free electorate and a just society. Both freedom and justice are in peril when fears of terrorism create political pressures for "security" beyond any realistic means of the government providing it.[10]

Rather than being naive about evil, we are willing to name it wherever it raises its ugly head, even when that means exposing U.S. actions and policies. It is because we take evil so seriously that we see evidence that too often decisions by government leaders are compromised by self-interests to the neglect of the common welfare. We see the integrity of the gospel being sacrificed in both the Christian Right's americanization of Christianity and its christianizing of America. It is a matter of conscience to speak out. To do otherwise would compromise our own integrity.

We strongly support Christian efforts to influence American politics. But those efforts must stop short of insisting that government legislate an exclusive Christian agenda. This is a balancing act wherein reason tempers passion, as Stephen Carter shows in his book, *The Culture of Disbelief*. As a constitutional law professor at Yale University and a practicing Christian, Carter is sympathetic to the role of religion in the political life of the nation. He says the Constitution goes beyond protection and provides accommodation to religious freedom. For this reason, he sees "the potential transformation of the Establishment Clause from a guardian of religious liberty into a guarantor of public secularism" as a "dismal and dreadful prospect."[11] The U. S. Supreme Court, he says, has never ruled that all accommodations are unconstitutional, but in general has ruled in favor of public religious expression. He cites the ruling allowing believers to wear religious apparel while on active military duty as one example.[12]

Carter also points out that the nature of religious conviction makes a clash between faith and state almost inevitable.

Constitutionally, religious groups are "intermediary" democratic institutions. This means they are autonomous, "not beholden to the secular world" and "unfettered in preaching resistance to (or support of or indifference toward) the existing order."[13] Thus, "religions are in effect independent centers of power, with bona fide claims on the allegiance of their members, claims that exist alongside, are not identical to, and will sometimes trump the claims to obedience that the state makes."[14]

But, to avoid religious tyranny in the public arena, Carter warns that Christians (and all religious adherents) must distinguish between (1) being motivated by one's faith to support a moral position the government can rightfully pursue and (2) simply oppressing members of other, less politically powerful faiths.[15] The latter leads to an effort to have the government sanction one's religious beliefs to the exclusion of others.

An example of this danger to which Carter points was a controversy in the state of Minnesota over a newly enacted piece of legislation requiring women to be given all available information related to abortion twenty-four hours prior to having one. Preliminary drafts of a state brochure and web site information stated that, contrary to some reports, a link between abortion and breast cancer was not supported by reliable medical studies. The final draft, however, changed the wording to read that some studies show there is no link while others suggest there is. Local news media uncovered the fact that the department had accepted information about this linkage from anti-abortion groups rather than the medical community itself. News reports also noted that career staff members within the department had argued against such politicizing of the web site because of the loss of credibility within the medical community that might result.[16] That is precisely what happened. Under a barrage of criticism, the department finally deleted the language suggesting a link between cancer and abortion, but then posted a minority report written by a lone individual who opposes abortion.

The above example underscores the excesses of the Christian Right at the expense of American democratic principles. It was not enough to win legislative approval of a bill that was not supported by public opinion polls. Basic medical information was politicized to further their agenda. This kind of behavior is why the role of religion has lost support among the American people. The issue is not tolerance of other points of view, as Carter notes. The Establishment Clause of the Constitution guarantees *religious equality*.

> The suggestion that those who are not Christian (or not Christians of the right kind) are merely tolerated— that they survive on these shores by forbearance, not by right—implies in turn that the folks in charge, the right-thinking Christians, can withdraw that tolerance at any time, thus destroying the political bases for the survival of all wrong-thinkers.[17]

Carter understands that this illustration could be reversed to apply to the notion that religious freedom is merely tolerated by a secular state. The final arbiter that prevents either from happening, he says, is *respect*. "If I tolerate you but do not respect you, the message of my tolerance...is that it is *my* forbearance, not *your* right, and certainly not *the nation's* commitment to equality, that frees you to practice your religion."[18]

Liberal Christians are willing to walk the thin line between moral convictions and respect for equality under the law. The Christian Right, on the other hand, does not show any sign of its willingness to do the same. We think the merging of their belief that America is a Christian nation and their conviction that their understanding of Christianity is the *only* religious truth lies behind their attitude.[19] Until they acknowledge the fact that the way they view church and state relations is *their* interpretation, not necessarily God's, there is little hope they will accept the principle of equality for all. The liberal Christian position is that *balance* is the key to protecting the integrity of religious convictions in the context of a democracy that fosters religious diversity and pluralism.

6

ENOUGH OF VENOMOUS ATTACKS

There is a mean spirit in America today, infecting our nation at many levels. It is a common malady among the most extreme political right wing pundits, as we document below. In addition, we will show that this same spirit has infected the Christian Right.

The San Francisco based radical right wing radio talk show host, Michael Savage, was fired by MSNBC after less than a six-month run of the television show they had created just for him.[1] Because of Savage's persistent, virulent attacks on minorities, homosexuals, liberals, and anyone else on his radar screen, the network had already received criticism for its decision to put him on the air. But it took an incident on the air for the folks at MSNBC finally to realize Savage was too savage for their own good. Something a caller on the weekend television show said sent Savage into orbit and on a verbal rampage.

> All right, so you're one of those sodomists. Are you a Sodomite? (Caller answers, "Yes, I am.") Oh, you're one of those Sodomites. You should get AIDS and die, you pig. How's that? Why don't you see if you can sue me, you pig? You got nothing better to do that put me down, you piece of garbage? You got nothing better to

do today? Go eat sausage and choke on it. Get trichinosis.[2]

This is an example of what fills the airwaves today from the radical right who are uncivil while claiming to serve the interests of their country. They wax on about the bias of a "liberal media" while dominating the talk show media. They ignore the fact that there are virtually no nationwide radio and television hosts whose sole purpose is to attack conservatives the way they attack liberals. The reality is that people like Savage are self-appointed political pundits who vent poison on radio and television for anyone and everyone to hear. This truly is genuine obscenity, yet the Christian Right remains silent in the face of it, busying itself with winning approval of legislation that requires libraries to install computer filters to prevent children from accessing "obscene" internet material.

The venomous attacking of liberals represents a new development in the political environment of this nation, with the potential to poison the entire system. It is distressing that the public seems to be in the mood to support it. Not only does Savage have a large radio following, he wrote a best-selling book filled with the same kind of hate talk that comes out of his mouth.

Savage is only one among many. No one uses venomous attacks better than Ann Coulter, about whom we have already made reference. She has perfected the habit of calling evil good and good evil. An attorney who got her start in the field of mean-spirited hyperbole by assisting Paula Jones in her lawsuit against Bill Clinton, Coulter targets anyone who disagrees with conservatives in general and with her in particular. Liberals, she charges, are guilty—get this—of the "politics of personal destruction."[3] Yet one is hard pressed to find a more abusive assault on people's character than what she writes in books and especially in her columns for the *Townhall*, an online ultra-conservative journal. From calling Ted Kennedy an "adulterous drunk" and Bill Clinton a "pervert, liar and a felon,"[4] she holds nothing back in her "seek and destroy" strategy. In a column defending the Falwell statement about 9/11 being God's judgment on this country because of gays and lesbians, Coulter wrote:

Walter Cronkite, better known as president of the Ho Chi Minh Veneration Society, has compared the Rev. Falwell to the Taliban. In response to Falwell's comment that gay marriage and abortion on demand may not have warmed the heart of the Almighty, Cronkite proclaimed it "the most abominable thing I've ever heard."

Showing the dispassion and critical judgment that earned him the moniker "the most pious blowhard in America," this self-serving, multimillionaire Martha's Vineyard boob accused Falwell of "worshiping the same God as the people who bombed the Trade Center and the Pentagon."

Liberals compare Jerry Falwell to the Taliban, but then are furious with George Bush for not being Jesus Christ.[5]

Coulter's views are so extreme they have reached the level of the absurd, charging that liberals are trying to destroy Christianity:

I don't know. Liberals have resisted Christianity pretty well. Christians are already a majority in America, and we can't even stop public school teachers from passing out condoms to fourth-graders or prevent Hollywood from producing movies that portray Christians as marauding skinheads.[6]

Writer Brenden Nyhan of Spinsanity.com, an online journal that promotes integrity and accuracy in public discourse, assesses Coulter's *Townhall* columns this way:

Coulter's world is cartoonish. Liberals are "terrorists" (1/11/01) and a "cult" (2/22/01) who "can never just make a principled argument" (3/22/01). Their arguments are portrayed as hysterical (2/9/01, 4/5/01, 6/15/01), screaming (1/18/01, 6/21/01) or starting political World War III (2/9/01, 3/8/01). Meanwhile, as Coulter depicts it, conservatives are being persecuted ceaselessly.

His analysis of her book, *Treason: Liberal Treachery from the Cold War to the War on Terrorism*,[7] is especially helpful in exposing the length to which she is willing to go to spew forth hatred for liberals. The fact that the book tries to make the case that the demagoguery of the late Senator Joseph McCarthy was nothing more than a liberal (meaning Democrat) attempt to smear a Republican who was telling the truth about communists infiltrating our government underscores the length to which people like Coulter will go in venting their attacks. The entire book is reflective of the paragraph below from one of her *TownHall* colums in which she defends McCarthy:

> The myth of "McCarthyism" is the greatest Orwellian fraud of our times. Liberals are fanatical liars, then as now. The portrayal of Sen. Joe McCarthy as a wild-eyed demagogue destroying innocent lives is sheer liberal hobgoblinism. Liberals weren't hiding under the bed during the McCarthy era. They were systematically undermining the nation's ability to defend itself, while waging a bellicose campaign of lies to blacken McCarthy's name. Liberals denounced McCarthy because they were afraid of getting caught, so they fought back like animals to hide their own collaboration with a regime as evil as the Nazis. As Whittaker Chambers said: "Innocence seldom utters outraged shrieks. Guilt does."[8]

Nyhan makes this assessment of the book:

> With her new book, syndicated pundit Ann Coulter has driven the national discourse to a new low. No longer content to merely call liberals "terrorists" or a "cult" who "hate democracy," she has now upped the ante, accusing the entire Democratic Party as well as liberals and leftists nationwide of treason. But, as in her syndicated columns (many of which are adapted in the book) and her previous book, *Slander: Liberal Lies Against the American Right,* Coulter's case relies in large part on irrational rhetoric and pervasive factual errors and deceptions.
>
> The accusation of treason is one of the most grave that can be made against a citizen of any country.

Article III of the U.S. Constitution specifies that "Treason against the United States, shall consist only in levying war against them, or in adhering to their enemies, giving them aid and comfort."

In latching onto a powerful word with a specific legal meaning and casually leveling the charge as a blanket accusation against a wide array of people (as she did with "slander"), Coulter is attempting to smear virtually anyone who disagrees with her views on foreign policy as treasonous.[9]

What, you may be asking yourself, does this have to do with the Christian Right? The answer is, just about everything. Outrageous personal attacks are as common among them as it is with the likes of Savage and Coulter. It seems political birds of a feather do flock together. In his reaction to the Supreme Court ruling that struck down the Texas sodomy law, for example, Pat Robertson wrote to his *The 700 Club* viewers. Calling his campaign, "Operation Supreme Court Freedom," he begins with a quote by Thomas Jefferson to the effect that believing the Supreme Court should serve as "the ultimate arbiter of constitutional interpretation," would be "a very dangerous doctrine indeed and one that would place us under the tyranny of an oligarchy" (no source or context cited). That Robertson speaks of the wisdom of Jefferson at all seems ironic since it is likely that were Jefferson alive today Robertson would consider him an enemy of God because of his non-Christian religious views.[10]

He uses the Jefferson quote as a backdrop for a litany of actions by the Supreme Court since 1962 that Robertson considers an attack on the "moral framework" of the United States itself. Among them are banning prayer, the Bible, the Ten Commandments, and statues of Jesus from public schools, buildings and parks; using a "right of privacy" not found in the Constitution to allow the slaughter of the unborn; declaring a constitutional right to consensual sodomy and, according to Robertson, opening the door to homosexual marriages, bigamy, legalized prostitution, and even incest.

Robertson then declares that the framers of the Constitution never intended anything like this to take place, and that we are now living under "the tyranny of a non-elected oligarchy.""Just think," he writes, "five unelected men and women who serve for life can change the moral fabric of our nation and take away the protections which our elected legislators have wisely put in place."

They will themselves be judged, he asserts in the same letter, by the "Judge of all the earth." Convinced that God will destroy America if its people continue to allow this ungodliness to go unchecked, Robertson tells his readers:

> In short, by its distorted reading of the religion clause of the First Amendment to the United States Constitution and its "discovery" of emanations from the Fourteenth Amendment called "penumbras," the Supreme Court is bringing upon this nation the wrath of God when the precious liberties that we love so much may be taken away from all of us.
>
> Would you join with me and many others in crying out to our Lord to change the Court? If we fast and pray and earnestly seek God's face, then He will hear our prayer and give us relief.
>
> One justice is 83 years old, another has cancer, and another has a heart condition. Would it not be possible for God to put it in the minds of these three judges that the time has come to retire? With their retirement and the appointment of conservative judges, a massive change in federal jurisprudence can take place.
>
> We can have a court that no longer legislates from the bench the wishes of *The New York Times* and *The Washington Post*, but which will earnestly seek to interpret the Constitution as it is written and to give meaning to the centuries of moral standards which have undergirded this wonderful country called the United States of America.
>
> Please join us in prayer to support a massive prayer offensive that we are going to call.[11]

Praying that Justices of the Supreme Court will soon die, a reasonable implication from Robertson's letter, oversteps the boundaries of civil discourse, not to mention the unchristian nature of such a prayer. How could any decent person not be shocked by this? When former Green Bay Packers coach Vince Lombardi said, "Winning isn't everything; it's the only thing," we don't believe he had the Christian Right in mind, but he certainly described their political strategy. And civility has been one of its casualties.

Incivility is not a new thing among the Christian Right. When Bill Clinton was elected President, Paul Weyrich, a right-wing republican who moves in Christian Right circles, declared, "The nation deserves the hatred of God under Clinton."[12] Not to be outdone, Jerry Falwell accused President Clinton of peddling drugs. Then through an organization called Citizens for Honest Government Falwell peddled *The Clinton Chronicles*, a video that claimed to have proof that Vincent Foster, the former White House deputy counsel, didn't commit suicide, but was murdered with Clinton's approval to keep him quiet about the Whitewater land deal in Arkansas.[13] This was the umbrella case investigated by the Republicans for eight years to no avail. Yet it allowed the "independent" counsel, Kenneth Starr, himself a Christian Righter, to expand the investigation that eventually led to the Clinton impeachment and exoneration.

Robertson devoted one of his *The 700 Club* broadcasts to addressing the question, "Suicide or Murder"—this, despite the fact that there was no truth to such claims and that the Christian Right was slandering the President of the United State. These are the same people who spin on about how the nation should stand behind its President in times of war, and are openly critical of those who criticized the war in Iraq and are now critical of the post-war mess the U.S. is currently facing. Letters of support for the President are still being sought on Christian Right web sites.[14]

What amazes us is the apparent ease with which the Christian Right uses venomous attacks on people with whom they disagree. During a 1992 battle against the Equal Rights Amendment, Robertson claimed that it advanced "a feminist agenda…that would encourage women to leave their husbands, kill their children, practice witchcraft, destroy capitalism, and become lesbian."[15] In his book, *The Coming New World Order*, Robertson claimed "the new world order," i.e., essentially the United Nations and everyone who supports it, "has been the code phrase of those who desired to destroy the Christian faith and what Pope Pius XI termed the 'Christian social order.' They wish to replace it with an occult-inspired world socialist dictatorship."[16] If that weren't enough, he later concludes: "The new world order will have as its religion a god of light, whom Bible scholars recognize as Lucifer. Nations who will walk in Lucifer's ways will find only suffering and heartache, but never peace!"[17]

More telling than the book, though, is the Christian Coalition he founded that vents venom against liberals whom they consider to be God haters, meaning anyone who supports abortion rights, affirmative action, equal pay for women, does not condemn homosexuality, or disagrees with any of Robertson's "pro-family" agenda.

As the "father" of the Christian Right, Jerry Falwell has shown through the years that he, too, is not hesitant to launch these kinds of attacks. In comments made September 12, 2001 in an appearance on Robertson's television show, *The 700 Club*, Falwell claimed that what happened the day before was the judgment of God on a nation awash in the sins of homosexuality, abortion, and everything else he deemed an abomination to God.

> I really believe that the pagans, and the abortionists, and the feminists, and the gays and the lesbians who are actively trying to make that an alternative lifestyle, the ACLU, People for the American Way—all of them who have tried to secularize America—I point the finger in their face and say, 'You helped this happen, the terrorist acts of September 11, 2001.'[18]

Falwell was greeted with a firestorm of criticism, forcing him later to say that he regretted what he said. Yet he also claimed the news media had taken his words out of context. Anyone who saw the telecast, however, or has since reviewed a tape of it, knows that no context was violated, that Falwell said what he said. Later, Robertson, who had responded to Falwell's statement by saying, "I totally concur," couldn't distance himself from Falwell fast enough.

But the cat was out of the bag. The statements of both men were consistent with the tone of the Christian Right since Falwell's founding of the Moral Majority. In a 1984 debate with gay activist Jerry Sloan, Falwell denied describing the gay-oriented Metropolitan Community Churches as "brute beasts" and "a vile and Satanic system" that will "one day be utterly annihilated and there will be a celebration in heaven." He went on to say that he would give Sloan $5000 if he could prove he ever said it. Sloan produced a tape to that effect. Falwell refused to pay up and Sloan sued and won. Falwell appealed, lost, and ended up paying an additional $2800. Here is what Falwell actually said:

> Look at the Metropolitan Community Church today, the gay church, almost accepted into the World Council of Churches. Almost, the vote was against them. But they will try again and again until they get in, and the tragedy is that they would get one vote. Because they are spoken of here in Jude as being brute beasts that is going to the baser lust of the flesh to live immorally, and so Jude describes this as apostasy. But thank God this vile and satanic system will one day be utterly annihilated and there'll be a celebration in heaven.

These words do not simply express a different point of view on the issue of homosexuality. They reveal a self-righteousness that lies beneath the Christian Right not being content to disagree with someone, but characterizing them as enemies of God.

During the 2003 legislative session, a Christian Right Minnesota state representative named Arlon Lindner made the charge that gays and lesbians were exaggerating Nazi persecution of homosexuals. His remarks were in support of his proposal to reverse a state law that makes it a crime to discriminate on the basis of sexual orientation. He believes the law promotes homosexuality among kids which, in his pattern of illogic, is spreading the gay disease, AIDS, which he also said was threatening to turn America into "another African continent."

Lindner's supporters, and there were many, claimed he was not a prejudiced man. Others, however, wondered how anyone with any sense of justice could believe that. It was not the first time this champion of the Christian Right had been in the news for disparaging comments about other people,[19] prompting an editorial in the Minneapolis *Star Tribune* to say of Lindner:

> Somewhere there must be a group Lindner hasn't insulted, a fact he hasn't ignored, a prejudice he hasn't embraced, a bizarre theory he hasn't espoused. But after his recent unsavory display, the list isn't easily conjured. The bill he's sponsoring is a bad one to begin with, and Lindner's conduct in promoting it has been shameful...
>
> Lindner has a right to say whatever offensive thing he wants. But the House has a right and a duty to denounce his views when he brings dishonor to the institution, as he so clearly has.[20]

Lindner wasn't fazed by any of the criticism he received, responding to demands for an immediate apology by saying, "I won't apologize for being right."[21]

That is one thing the Christian Right says that is most often true. They won't apologize. They are never sorry for what they actually say, only that they are sorry when someone gets offended. That is as close to an apology as they get. Saying you are sorry for what you said means you made a mistake, and that is not something for which the Christian Right believes it is ever guilty.

Yet even with numerous examples of how extreme the Christian Right is, liberal Christians have thus far been less than attentive to the danger they pose. We have failed to understand that their mean spirited attacks are not the result of a momentary loss of control, but reflect a strategy for winning the battle, as clinical psychologist Andrew Weaver documents in an article about the Christian Right's targeting of United Methodists, Presbyterians, and Episcopalians for takeover:

> Irving Kristol, father of William Kristol, editor of *The Weekly Standard* and one of the "godfathers" of the political right, summed up this strategy in *The Wall Street Journal*: "Attack the integrity, not the words, of

those with whom you disagree." More recently, Grover Norquist, a conservative activist and long-time friend of top presidential aide Karl Rove, was even more blunt when he told *The Denver Post* that civility is out and nastiness is in among conservative activists. According to Mr. Norquist, "bipartisanship" is another name for date rape.[22]

Weaver also cites journalist Leon Howell's book, *United Methodism at Risk: A Wake Up Call,* that suggests liberal Christians thus far have not shown the temperament to meet the challenge of the Christian Right:

> Methodists and other mainstream Protestants have held proudly to the "extreme middle" during most of their history, recognizing that self-righteousness is the bane of religion, be it the ideology of the left or right. Unless progressive and moderate members in the mainline churches muster the will to organize and battle for what they believe is fair and just, they are in danger of losing the historical values of these traditions to a determined cadre of ideological advocacy groups. It is time, in other words, for "fighting Methodists" to make a comeback lest their tolerance and Christian charity be turned against them and used to undermine their churches and further the social ends of the right wing's radical ideology.[23]

This book is our effort to show we are up to the task. We do not deceive ourselves in thinking that the Christian Right will stop their personal attacks. But we are hopeful that in saying we have had enough, others might be encouraged to say the same thing. Perhaps a ground swell of "enough" would send a message to politicians of every stripe that the politics of personal destruction is a strategy that is not tolerable in a civil society, and certainly not in Christian circles!

7

ENOUGH OF BAPTIZED PARTISAN POLITICS

When Senator Rick Santorum (R-PA) declared that homosexuals were dangerous to American society, Roberta Combs, executive director of the Christian Coalition, had this to say about the criticism he received.

> Bankrupt of positive ideas, liberals pursue this issue in the hope of attention with exaggerated explanations of Senator Santorum's statement. Democratic politicians and the left-wing press should be ashamed for inhibiting freedom of speech. Homosexuality clearly is an alternative lifestyle. We stand with, and support, Senator Santorum.

Despite the fact that many of his republican colleagues were critical of Santorum's comments, Ms. Combs still chose to accuse Democrats of making something out of nothing. Not surprising, since the political power base for the Christian Right's drive to govern America is the radical right wing of the Republican Party. This does not mean that all Republicans are members of the Christian Right. In point of fact, more than a few are disturbed by the Christian Right's views and actions, and displeased with their Republican colleagues who have fallen in step with them or cater to them to win elections.

There is nothing inherently wrong with the political marriage of fundamentalist Christians and Republicans. Labor unions have traditionally been Democratic. On the other hand, there is nothing particularly right about such an alliance, and that is our point! Political action groups are an example of democracy at work. What bothers us is the fact that the Christian Right identifies Christianity with Republican views and Republican candidates. Many Republicans are Christian. So are liberal Democrats, Independents, and others who disagree with the Christian Right, something Ms. Combs apparently does not believe.

Some Christian Right members make no bones about their partisanship. Pat Robertson and Gary Bauer sought the Republican nomination for president in the 1988 and 2000 primaries. Former executive director of Robertson's Christian Coalition, Ralph Reed, is now a Republican consultant. Every politician David Limbaugh cites as a true Christian just happens to be a Republican, and every liberal politician waging war against Christianity just happens to be a Democrat. He goes to great lengths in defending Tom Delay of Texas, one of the most arrogant and divisive politicians this nation has seen in a generation.[1] Jerry Falwell is an open supporter of Republican presidential candidates, and recently commented that he didn't see how any Democrat could be a Christian.[2] James Dobson, who claims to be non-partisan, is described by Gil Alexander-Moegerle, co-founder of Focus on the Family, in this way.

> Dobson's agenda is so thoroughly Republican and so thoroughly antithetical to the perspectives of the Democratic Party that his frequent attempts to suggest that he is somehow a political eunuch are transparently thin and often humorous.[3]

One way the Christian Right shows its partisanship most clearly is in its voter registration and sample ballot drives. These are some of their past activities:

Before the 2000 presidential election, Falwell organized the "People of Faith 2000" campaign. By his own admission, the project's purpose was registering and mobilizing voters to benefit Bush and other Republican candidates. In the 2000 election, the Christian Coalition participated in the following activities:

(1) Distributed a self-proclaimed record 70 million voter guides throughout the United States slanted to steer conservative Christian voters to Bush and the GOP;
(2) Registered voters;
(3) Made automated phone calls to voters;
(4) Launched "21 Victory," an election-year project to raise funds;
(5) Hosted its own political rally with pro-Bush speakers, had Bush speak at the Coalition's annual "Road To Victory" conference in Washington;
(6) Mailed thousands of postcards in key battleground states; and,
(7) Hosted a series of "God and Country" rallies to promote the pro-Bush voter guides.[4]

Other examples of the Christian Right's identification of Republican views with Christianity include:

•Falwell recently complained that "deceitful" Senate Democrats were holding hostage President Bush's nomination of Miguel Estrada to the Second Circuit Court of Appeals in Washington, D.C., who finally withdrew from consideration.[5] A page on Robertson's Christian Coalition web site, the political action group founded by Pat Robertson in 1989, contains similar criticism of Democrats on this issue. Yet not once did either of them raise a question about Senate Republicans refusing to bring Clinton judicial nominations to a vote or Senator Jesse Helm's holding ambassadorial appointments hostage to his own homophobia.

•The Christian Coalition's Web site is better than the Republican Party's own site in promoting a Republican agenda. During the Iraqi war it contained a "support the president" letter people could sign that was sent to Mr. Bush informing him of the Christian Coalition's support for the war.

•Robertson's legal arm, the Center for Justice and Peace, has been a strong advocate for the administration's challenge to the affirmative action practices of the University of Michigan

Law School.[6] It seems lost on Robertson and Bush that both of them have benefited from "affirmative action for the well-to-do" (as sons of prominent political leaders).

•The Family News Focus area of James Dobson's Focus on the Family web site "reported" on the case before the U.S. Supreme Court challenging the sodomy law of the state of Texas[7] with its Washington correspondent, David Brody, quoting Jordan Lorence, senior counsel at the Alliance Defense Fund, as saying, "I think it was a sad day for the republic that this question is even before the court." Lorence is then quoted as adding, "People need to be praying for the Supreme Court to come to the right decision and not give constitutional protection to homosexual activity," Lorence said.[8]

•Regarding Mr. Bush's judicial nominees, Brody "reported," "Liberals unveil yet another plan to keep President Bush from appointing federal judges. On Capitol Hill, there is another indication that liberal Democrats are playing political hardball with President Bush's judicial nominees."[9]

•Regarding the Estrada nomination, Brody wrote, "Add to the list nominee Jeffrey Sutton, bringing the total to five nominees rejected outright. Republicans believe liberals won't be able to pull off multiple filibusters without looking like obstructionists. John Nowacki, who monitors judicial nominations for the Free Congress Foundation, said this has to do with Democrats believing the true President is not in office. One senator, not long ago, said this is motivated by spite. 'I think that's absolutely right,' Nowacki said, adding that what bothers Democrats is the idea that Bush is appointing judges and not Al Gore."[10]

In an effort to have a freer hand in promoting Republican candidates for the 2004 election, the Christian Right is working hard for the Houses of Worship Free Speech Restoration Act (H.R. 235), proposed by Rep. Walter Jones, R-N.C. and endorsed by 156 members. This bill "amends the Internal Revenue Code to state that churches and other houses of worship shall not lose such designation because of the content, preparation, or presentation of any homily, sermon, teaching, dialectic, or other presentation made during religious services or gatherings." In other words, houses of worship could campaign on behalf of specific candidates without losing their tax-exempt status as long as such participation did not become a substantial part of the institution's activity.[11]

Again, we are not concerned that Christian Right leaders support and endorse Republican candidates. It's their claim that they do so out of a *Christian* obligation that offends us. Christians have as much right to hold political office and wield political power as anyone. But when the line between neo-conservative Republican party views and Christianity is blurred, religion and politics become mixed in a destructive way. At the heart of the problem is the Christian Right's failure to distinguish between theological and political conservatism. It chooses, rather, to wrap itself and the Bible in an American flag and call the package Republican.[12]

The Christian Right's ideological enemy may be liberalism, but the only conclusion one can reach when examining the record is that Democrats are the human face of liberalism the Right believes is anti-God. Thus, the Republican Party is their party, and by implication, God's party as well. Moreover, the Republican Party has become their primary venue for winning political victories they could not win as a group unto themselves. Social critic and writer Wendy Kaminer says, the power of the Christian Right is "not exercised through previously prominent interest groups like the Christian Coalition or the Moral majority." Rather, she says, their perspectives "have been incorporated into the Republican Party. So while its organizations appear to be in decline, the Christian Right has more political power than ever. You don't need lobbying groups to petition the government when your cohort runs the government."[13]

The key person in this partnership between the Christian Right and the Republican Party is President Bush. Kaminer points out how he has been skillful in making this alliance quite subtle by promoting an image of religious tolerance. Thus, "under his leadership, right-wing Christianity seems more likely to be associated with compassionate conservativism than mean fundamentalism."[14] But, she says, the effect is the same. "Christian conservatives now help shape a broad range of government policies, especially on the domestic front, in the areas of science, social policy, and social services. The president repeatedly refers to the power of faith to cure social ills, and examples of sectarian policy making, or grant-making abound."[15]

It is possible that God has chosen the Republican Party to lead America back to its "Christian" roots. But those of us who are liberal Christians do not believe it. Instead, we believe that the partisan nature of the Christian Right's agenda is precisely why their claim to be speaking for God is bogus. It is arrogant to the core and lacks credibility. They speak for themselves and in that regard have every right to do so. But they do not speak for God. They speak only for themselves. That makes their views political. Whether or not they are Christian is a point of controversy, hardly an established fact. If they want to be taken seriously as prophets of faith rather than political partisans, they need to lose the partisan politics they have thus far displayed. At the same time, baptizing partisanship could be diminished if Republican Party leaders who disagree with the Christian Right would disassociate themselves from its leaders when they promote policies and actions that compromise the separation of church and state.

Partisan politics has become dirty business in this country. Perhaps it always has been, but there was a modicum of "honor" even among these "thieves." That has all but dissipated now, due in no small measure to the Christian Right. It has helped to poison the political climate through its personal attacks on the faith and character of Democrats, going back to the time when Falwell condemned candidate Jimmy Carter for giving an interview to *Playboy*. He didn't address Carter's position on issues. He questioned his being a Christian for granting the interview itself. This has been the tone of Christian Right attacks, and has now become the tone of political debate in general. It is time for all people of faith, and especially Christian politicians, to say enough is enough to this radical group of religious zealots who give both Christianity and politics a bad name.

8

ENOUGH OF BLIND NATIONALISM

Just when you thought it couldn't get worse, it does. As bad as the Christian Right's christianizing of America and baptizing partisan politics are, the support both provide for blind nationalism borders on outright idolatry. By nationalism we mean "devotion to the interests or culture of a particular nation and the promotion of its interests above those of all other nations."[1] We are not suggesting that such devotion is wrong or unwarranted. Every nation needs such commitment to national ideals and the policies that promote them in order to form an effective union and government. Our concern is that uncritical devotion to any nation invites injustice and may indirectly promote tyranny. For Christians this blindness skews the relationship between what belongs to Caesar and what belongs to God. When Jesus said emperors were entitled to receive their due (Matthew 22:21), he was not suggesting they are equal to God. It is the failure of the Christian Right to maintain this distinction that troubles us. A true story illustrates why.

Ebehard Bethge and his wife, Renata, were German Christians during the Third Reich. She was the niece of German theologian Dietrich Bonhoeffer, who was executed by Hitler for his resistance to Nazism. Dr. Bethge was Bonhoeffer's closest friend. In the early 1980's the Bethges were scholars-in-residence at Lynchburg College in Virginia during my tenure there as College Chaplain. They attended Falwell's Thomas Road Baptist Church soon after their arrival. When they walked in, an usher immediately and without their permission pinned a Christian flag on one of Dr. Bethge's coat lapels and an American flag on the other. Having lived through the tragedy of the German Church refusing to resist Hitler, and being forced to go underground as a member of the Confessing Church of Germany that did resist, the Bethges were extremely disturbed by this action. On numerous occasions thereafter Dr. Bethge told audiences of this experience and then he would ask, "Do you know what happens when these two are put together?" pointing to both flags. Moving his finger to the lapel on which the American flag had been placed he would say, "This one always wins!"

Perhaps the lessons of the Holocaust have been lost on the Christian Right. Jesus was quite clear in his denunciation of any attempt by covenant people to put God in a box as if they can define who God is or who constitute the people of God. Israel (and later the early church) repeatedly blurred the distinction between covenant and privilege. By the time of Jesus, living under oppressive foreign powers for five hundred years had fueled a radical nationalistic zeal among members of the first-century Jewish community.[2] The New Testament Gospel of Luke records an incident of Jesus' giving a sermon in his hometown congregation in Nazareth at the beginning of his ministry that reveals how strong it actually was (Luke 4:16–30).

In essence, to the people gathered Jesus said that God cared about Jews and non-Jews alike, not something one would think would be so controversial as it turned out to be. When he illustrated his point with two stories from their tradition— one about Elijah being sent by God to give food to a non-Israelite woman and her son during a famine in Israel, the other about God sending Elisha to heal Naaman, the Captain of the Syrian Army, who was suffering from leprosy at a time when there were many lepers in Israel—the people became enraged and were ready to throw him off a cliff.[3]

We believe the Christian Right would have reacted to Jesus the way the people in the story did. We do not see any indication that they believe God is bigger than what *they* believe about God, or that God is free to bless whomever God chooses to bless, whether they like it or not. They tend to be more American than Christian in the way they see the world. Unfortunately they are not alone, as a poll taken during the 2003 war with Iraq by the Pew Research Center and the Pew Forum on Religion and Public Life confirmed. It found that the views on the war among most American Christians were more influenced by family, the news media, and political affiliation than by what they heard from religious leaders. Only one-in-ten Americans said their personal religious beliefs were the most influential on their views and only one-in-five of those who attend church weekly.[4]

This survey suggests it is likely the Christian Right is not alone in its uncritical support of the policies and actions of our government. The "my country, love it or leave it" mentality is not a new phenomenon. This is the very reason the damage the Christian Right does in its blind nationalism must be taken so seriously. Christianity should not be used to justify American policies that are shaped by the same kind of self-interests that guide the policies of other nations. Moreover, the fact that President Bush uses "good verses evil" language to foster support for his policies—something he has frequently done since 9/11—does not help the situation. In short, the President's speeches have been laced with an ideology of America as good and all our enemies as evil, so much so that his foreign policy has been described as "evangelical."[5]

His "axis of evil" State of the Union address in 2002 epitomizes the kind of blind nationalism we are talking about. By characterizing other nations as "evil," the inference to America as "righteous" was inescapable. A national audience heard this speech as a call for America to take up the mantle of fighting against evil because God has so destined us with this responsibility. In a speech on September 11, 2002 marking one year after the Twin Towers and Pentagon attacks, the President made a similar reference to the righteousness of our cause.

> Tomorrow is September 12. A milestone is passed, and a mission goes on. Be confident. And our country is

strong. And our cause is even larger than our country. Ours is the cause of human dignity: freedom guided by conscience and guarded by peace. This ideal of America is the hope of all mankind. That hope drew millions to this harbor. That hope still lights our way. And the light shines in the darkness. And the darkness will not overcome it.

It may have gone unnoticed by most Americans, if not most Christians, but the last two lines are a paraphrase of a biblical text from the Gospel of John: "and the life was the light of all people. The light shines in the darkness, and the darkness did not overcome it" (1:4). The biblical reference is to Jesus being the light of the world. In the paraphrase the Bush speechwriter replaced Jesus with American ideals, and by implication, the Bush policies that supposedly express them.

But, of course, Mr. Bush had already set the theological tone of his war on terrorism when he spoke to the nation shortly after 9/11 happened.

I will not forget this wound to our country or those who inflicted it. I will not yield; I will not rest; I will not relent in waging this struggle for freedom and security for the American people.

The course of this conflict is not known, yet its outcome is certain. Freedom and fear, justice and cruelty, have always been at war, and we know that God is not neutral between them. (Applause.)

Fellow citizens, we'll meet violence with patient justice—assured of the rightness of our cause, and confident of the victories to come. In all that lies before us, may God grant us wisdom, and may He watch over the United States of America.

His words seem innocent enough, especially at a time of such horrific grief and shock because of what had happened. But upon close examination their real meaning is obvious. God is on the side of American democracy, which is why God will watch over us as a nation. While he has insisted the war on terrorism is not aimed at Islam, his words have encouraged the Christian Right to think this way. The recent comments by Lt. Gen. William G. "Jerry" Boykin, Deputy Undersecretary of Defense for Intelligence and a much-decorated and twice-wounded veteran, are a case in point. Boykin participated in covert military operations including a clash with Muslim warlords in Somalia, the hunt for Colombian drug czar Pablo Escobar, and the attempted rescue of American hostages in Iran in 1980. Boykin is also a fundamentalist Christian who thinks the war on terrorism is in fact a battle between Christianity and Islam. Actually, he believes the war is between the God of Christians and the lesser god of Muslims, as the following excerpts from some of his speeches illustrate (the specific fundamentalist Christian audiences are in parentheses):

> And we ask ourselves this question, "Why do they hate us? Why do they hate us so much?" Ladies and gentlemen, the answer to that is because we're a Christian nation, because our foundation and our roots are Judeo-Christian. Did I say Judeo-Christian? Yes. Judeo-Christian.
>
> That means we've got a commitment to Israel. That means it's a commitment we're never going to abandon. Go back and read the history books. Go back and read what the early founders of this nation said about Israel, about the Jews. John Adams wrote extensively of, he called it the Hebrews, the contributions they had made to our concepts of liberty and the importance of their contributions to the founding of this great nation.
>
> Thomas Jefferson and Benjamin Franklin each, independently, when asked to come up with a national symbol for this new nation, both came up with a national symbol that reflected on our Jewish heritage. One had Moses standing over the Red Sea with his staff and the water parting. The other had the Israelites coming out of bondage in the desert being led by a ball of fire. They recognized the importance of our relationship to the Jews and to Israel. Ladies and gentlemen, we will never abandon Israel, we will never

walk away from our commitment to Israel because our roots are there.

Our religion came from Judaism, and therefore these radicals will hate us forever. *(Spoken at Good Shepherd Church, Sandy, Oregon, June 21, 2003, during a Celebrate America event.)*

There was a man in Mogadishu named Osman Atto. You see him in the movie [*Blackhawk Down*], smoking a big cigar and talking philosophically. How many of you have seen the movie? Acting like a big shot. Well let me tell you something. That's not what Osman Atto did. The reality was Osman Atto was Aideed's [Somalian warlord] closest ally. He was Aideed's top lieutenant. He was a multimillionaire financier for Aideed's clan. And we knew that if we could capture Osman Atto and take him away, that we could destroy Aideed's network. So we went after Osman Atto about two weeks before the battle...We went after Osman Atto. We got into a terrible fight. And I'm sad to say a lot of Somalis were killed as we went after Osman Atto. But we missed him by seconds. He walked out of the facility that we raided, he walked down the street and blended in with the crowd and we missed him. And then he went on CNN and he laughed at us, and he said, 'They'll never get me because Allah will protect me. Allah will protect me."

Well, you know what? I knew that my God was bigger than his. I knew that my God was a real God, and his was an idol. But I prayed, Lord, let us get that man. Three days later we went after him again, and this time we got him. Not a mark on him. We got him. We brought him back into our base there and we had a Sea Land container set up to hold prisoners in, and I said, "Put him in there." They put him in there, there was one guard with him. I said, "Search him." They searched him, and then I walked in with no one in there but the guard, and I looked at him and said, "Are you Osman Atto?" And he said "Yes." And I said, "Mr. Atto, you underestimated our God." *(Delivered at First Baptist Church, Daytona, Florida, January 28, 2003)*

In all his presentations, General Boykin used slides to make his points more dramatic. In the excerpt below, he begins with a slide showing Osama bin Laden.

> And then we began to see this face…the face of Osama bin Laden. And finally we said, "There's the enemy. That's our enemy. That's the man that hates us. And all of those that follow him [Jesus]."
>
> (Picture of President Bush) And then this man stepped forward. A man that has acknowledged that he prays in the Oval Office. A man that's in the White House today because of a miracle. You think about how he got in the White House. You think about why he's there today. As Mordecai said to Esther, "You have been put there for today." As Mordecai said to Esther, "You have been put there for such a time and place." And this man has been put in the White house to lead our nation in such a time as this.
>
> But who is that enemy? It's not Osama bin Laden. Our enemy is a spiritual enemy because we are a nation of believers. You go back and look at our history, and you will find that we were founded on faith. Look at what the writers of our Constitution said. We are a nation of believers. We were founded on faith.
>
> (Picture of Satan) And the enemy that has come against our nation is a spiritual enemy. His name is Satan. And if you do not believe that Satan is real, you are ignoring the same Bible that tells you about God. Now I'm a warrior. One day I'm going to take off this uniform and I'm still going to be a warrior. And what I'm here to do today is to recruit you to be warriors of God's kingdom. *(First Baptist Church, Broken Arrow, Oklahoma, June 23, 2003)*

The response of the Christian Right has been to defend the General on his combat record and charge his critics with intolerance. This is a common tactic of the Christian Right.

Criticize them for self-righteousness and they accuse you of intolerance. The question we want answered is why the Christian Right would presume there is any biblical basis for believing God is a Christian or that God watches over this nation more than others. Scripture is unequivocal in its insistence that neither religious nor national loyalties and boundaries can define the God of Israel and Jesus. We believe any attempt to use scripture to do so is idolatrous. History shows that unbridled nationalism always leads to disastrous consequences.

We affirm the response of Jim Wallis of *Sojourners* magazine when he wrote a public letter to Boykin questioning the General's understanding of the Bible.

> But I want to raise some…issues: biblical theology, bad teaching, and church discipline. General, your theology bears no resemblance to biblical teaching. You utterly confuse the body of Christ with the American nation. The kingdom of God doesn't endorse the principalities and powers of nation-states, armies, and the ideologies of empire; but rather calls them all into question. You even miss the third verse of "Onward Christian Soldiers," which reminds us, "Crowns and thrones may perish, Kingdoms rise and wane, But the Church of Jesus, constant will remain." And let's not misinterpret the famous first verse, "Onward Christian soldiers marching *as* to war, with the *cross* of Jesus going on before." The cross, General, not the Special Forces.[6]

It would seem the attitude of the Christian Right in regard to its support of America proves the adage that the only thing we learn from history is that we don't learn from it. The Barmen Declaration of 1933 that declared Jesus Christ is the only head of the church and not the state was in reaction to the nationalism of the official state Church of Germany that chose to remain silent in the face of rising German nationalism. The danger of Christians "losing their souls" whenever they allow nationalism to permeate their thinking is so obvious that it is simply astounding that the Christian Right does not understand what they are doing.

The church's support of German nationalism that led to the Holocaust is only one example of the damage done when the line between Christianity and patriotism becomes indistinguishable. Pages of European history are filled with examples of injustice, oppression, and war born of the collusion between church and state. During the days of apartheid in South Africa, the Dutch Reform Church gave support to one of the worst racist systems of government the world has known. American history is not a clean slate either. Soon after the colonies were settled, religious oppression raised its ugly head. Clergy in the new world often preached that America was "the Righteous Empire" in justifying westward expansion and destruction of native American culture.[7]

The Christian Right apparently chooses to ignore history and allows their politics to cloud their judgment about what is appropriate in the relationship between God and country. The actions and policies of our government today cry out for "prophetic critique" from the Christian community. In his book, *Is Religion Killing Us?* Jack Nelson-Pallmeyer describes how he engages audiences in an exercise that graphically drives this point home.

He begins by asking the audience what happened on September 11, 2001. Everyone knows the answer. Then he asks them what happened on September 11, 1973. No one knows. He then tells them that on that date the U.S. sponsored the overthrow of Chilean President, Salvador Allende. Allende had come to power through democratic elections. But Henry Kissinger did not believe his election served American interests. The coup replaced Allende with General Augusto Pinochet who was pro-American and whose regime became infamous for its brutality and murder of civilians who opposed his dictatorship.[8]

Nelson-Pallmeyer also asks the group how many people died on September 11, 2001. The answer is some 3000. He then tells them that while it is right that we grieve the deaths of those killed that day, we should also grieve the fact that more civilians died as a result of our U.S. bombing of Afghanistan than on 9/11. According to the Food and Agricultural Organization of the United Nations, more than 35,000 children died of hunger the day of the terrorist attacks.[9]

Finally Nelson-Pallmeyer asks his audience about December 7, 1941. Most of them know it was the day Pearl Harbor was bombed. Then he asks what happened on December 7, 1975. No one responds. He proceeds to tell them that this was the day more than 200,000 people were slaughtered in East Timor by Indonesian troops using U.S. weapons and with the expressed approval of the then Ford Administration.[10]

This material is not intended to say that America is an evil nation. It simply points out why the Christian Right's support of American policies is a de facto "Christian" endorsement of the notion that America is a righteous nation and, thus, is exempt from the kind of scrutiny to which we subject other nations. The Christian Right may couch their rhetoric in the guise of threats to the moral fiber of the nation, but when all is said and done their religious language disguises a dangerous nationalism and represents a clear and present danger to the nation and the integrity of Christianity.

For liberal Christians, placing the American flag in churches is an alarming practice. It blurs the line between appropriate patriotism and idolatrous nationalism. Worse, it ignores the essential distinction between God and country. "The flag," says Christian layman Manish Nandy, a former World Bank official and U.S. diplomat in Central America, "is a political symbol. It tells us of a people's admiration for a country, their valuation of that country over all others, their supreme allegiance to their own land. Like a company logo, it is a shorthand statement of the user's adherence to its goals and values."[11] He then goes to the heart of the issue by asking, "Is this what we should place inside our church?"

In the remainder of the article, Nandy details why flags have no place in churches. For one thing, "a sanctuary is a place for worship and not for economics or politics." For another, "the flag conveys a message of exclusivism, of a geographically located group apart from other groups." Finally, and in his opinion most serious, is that "a flag in a church conveys a message of prioritization: The nationals have a special claim to that house of God," as for example, the fact that the stars and stripes displayed in a church says in effect that while all people are equal, "Americans are more equal than others."[12]

Nandy then points out that the flaunting of the flag in churches is more egregious here in the U.S. than any other country in the world. His concluding statement captures the heart and mind of liberal Christians who desire to balance being American with being Christian:

> As U.S. diplomats, my wife and I have risked our lives—and those of our children—for our flag in troubled countries. I would find it intolerable to be accused of insufficient attachment to the flag. I find it just as intolerable to find the flag placed in my church, something that intrudes on my faith and on my sense of political propriety.[13]

This is the position liberal Christians must take in how we relate to our government. Thinking this way means we generally find ourselves being labeled anti-God, unpatriotic, and even aiding and abetting U.S. enemies. Further, we realize our views may not have any immediate impact on the climate of this nation, political or religious, in the near term. That does not weaken our resolve to continue efforts to expose the Christian Right's support of blind American nationalism that is souring our relations with other nations, and in the process is undercutting the very faith the Right claims to want to protect and preserve.

9

ENOUGH OF HYPOCRISY

The Book of Virtues guru, William Bennett, has admitted to a compulsion for gambling involving eight million dollars he earned from telling others how to be virtuous. In his own defense, he says he hasn't committed any crime so what he does with his own money is nobody's business.

All well and good, unless you've been playing the moral policeman for the nation. Then what you do with your money and your life *is* other people's business. It's called "credibility," and its counterpart is "hypocrisy." The Christian Right has never shown much concern for either, as the Bennett story graphically illustrates. As Katha Pollitt observed when the news about Bennett the gambler broke:

> Bennett's defenders make much of the fact that he never condemned gambling and so was not actually a hypocrite. Leaving your own pet vice off a long, long list of sins, and then, when you are found out, exempting that vice as practiced by you but not as practiced by others—that's not exculpation from charges of hypocrisy, that's what hypocrisy *is*.

Pollitt then names the real problem:

> If Bennett were a jolly, modest fellow, full of love for fallen humanity and the first to admit he was just

another sinner like the rest of us—if he were less quick to impute the worst motives to perfectly ordinary behavior, like having two kids; if he spent less time promoting rigid, puritanical morals and more time promoting, oh, kindness and tolerance and looking into your own heart and cutting other people some slack because you never really know what demons they're contending with—no one would be piling on now.

But then, with a message like that, no one would have heard of him in the first place. You don't get to play Christian on TV, or amass real political power along with your millions, by urging people not to throw the first stone, especially if they live in a glass house. Jesus tried that, and look what happened to him.[1]

Apparently members of the Christian Right don't know their feet are made of the same clay as everyone else's. They seem also to have forgotten the verse in the Bible that says, "When pride comes, then comes disgrace" (Proverbs 11:2). Hypocrisy is born of pride and arrogance.

I personally had seen the disregard for humility or integrity long before our group decided enough was enough. Actually I had seen enough twenty years before when I left my position as a college chaplain in Lynchburg, Virginia. More than a few people in my hometown viewed Falwell with disdain and disgust. This is a man who, while damning others for immorality, established his Lynchburg Christian Academy as a segregated alternative to an integrated public school system. Rather than finally admitting his mistake, though, he has chosen to compound his hypocrisy by denying what he did.[2]

One of the unpleasantries endemic to living in Falwell land, as his power and influence began to rise, was the parade of reporters and freelance writers from around the country wanting to talk to anyone who would talk about Falwell. It was a hot topic and they knew they could sell their stories to magazines and journals. It didn't take long for the natives to grow restless because of the fascination the rest of the country seemed to have with him. I didn't leave Lynchburg because of Falwell, but I confess to no small relief in not being in daily earshot of him.

But he followed me everywhere I went. Not directly, but he was in the news no matter where ministry took me. The Reagan years were good to Falwell and the Christian Right. Whether Reagan agreed with Falwell or simply used him is known only to those closest to him, but there is no doubt that Falwell used Reagan to advance his own interests. A small southern town preacher dining at the White House was big stuff. It took the Reagan White House to move Falwell from a local moral crusader to a national one. When the Reagan years ended, Falwell said that he was going to turn his attention to preaching the gospel. Then Bill Clinton got elected and Falwell chose to come out of "political" retirement. It was during the Clinton presidency that the Christian Right's hypocrisy became downright fanatical.

One of the most appalling examples of Christian Right hypocrisy was exposed in an article about Robertson's business connections with the now deposed Liberian President Charles Taylor. Taylor was a warlord who treated his own people as horribly as Saddam Hussein treated Iraqis. In 1992 he was also responsible for the murder of five American citizens, but was never brought to justice. They were Catholic nuns from Illinois working with the poor in the Liberian city of Monrovia. The story of their slaughter, based on eyewitness accounts, was provided by retired Foreign Service officer Gerald Rose, who was deputy chief of mission at the American Embassy in Liberia during the days of fighting in 1991-93, and the congressional testimony of Sister Stephanie Mertens, peace and justice coordinator of the Adorers of the Blood of Christ religious order to which the five slain nuns belonged.

Taylor's "boy soldiers," as they were called because they were mostly teenagers, ordered all occupants of the convent in Gardensville, a suburb of Monrovia, into the streets. They screamed that they would kill everyone who was white. Sister Kathleen was shot in front of the children, first in the arm, then in the head. Sister Shirley, a math teacher, and Sister Agnes, a nurse, were next. Sisters Kolmer and Muttra had left the convent three days earlier to drive their worried security guard to his home where he could be reunited with his family. They never made it. Their car was ambushed and everyone was murdered.

The American Embassy later found the decomposed bodies of the two nuns and the security guard covered with tarpaulins outside their car, and the partially decomposed bodies of the other three nuns in Gardensville, lying where they had been shot.

These murders, along with all of his other crimes against humanity, provide a context for Robertson's business dealings with Taylor, as told by Colbert King in a 2001 article in *The Washington Post*.

A few years after American Embassy staff stood on an airport tarmac in Liberia to bid a sad farewell to the five dead Americans, Pat Robertson signed an agreement with Charles Taylor allowing Robertson's for-profit company, Freedom Gold, to start a mining venture in southeastern Liberia. The deal gives Taylor's regime 10 percent ownership of the company, not including royalties and rental fees that it will pocket when the mining venture gets rolling.

Now draw near to hear what conservative Orange County, Calif., Republican Rep. and House Africa subcommittee chairman Ed Royce had to say about Taylor during a public hearing this year: "Charles Taylor has waged a continuous assault on the democratic dreams of the Liberian people. He rules by decree, he suppresses the press…and he sanctions, if not directs, the murder of political opponents. He and his so-called 'inner circle' control virtually all the nation's significant trade…Liberia has been described as Charles Taylor Inc. This corporation is corrupt to its core."

The subcommittee's ranking Democrat and Congressional Black Caucus member Donald Payne of New Jersey spoke about Taylor's arrest of journalists and human rights activists who "are working to document the government's terrible human rights record. Late last year, a leading pro-democracy group was attacked by a group of armed thugs as police watched," Payne said.

Speaking of the deal they cut, Robertson wrote to Taylor two years ago, "I pray that this investment may become a wonderful blessing to the people of Liberia and will be one of many significant investments that will be made under your administration in the nation of Liberia."[3]

It is this kind of story that makes liberal Christians wonder how Robertson has the temerity to lecture the nation on morality. Yet it is simply the tip of the Christian Right iceberg. What seems to drive them is not commitment to truth or Christian values, but a zeal that has dulled their conscience.

Another damning revelation of the kind of hypocrisy is David Brock's book, *Blinded by the Right*.[4] Indeed, this book offers an insider's perspective of just how widespread the hypocrisy is among them. Brock is the conservative writer who championed the cause of Clarence Thomas when he was charged with sexual misconduct by Anita Hill during his Supreme Court confirmation hearings. His book, *The Real Anita Hill*, became a bestseller and put Brock in the forefront of radical right journalism. He admits that he distorted the truth about Anita Hill's personal life to serve a political purpose and to further his own career. In fact, Brock writes that since the hearings, he has found sufficient evidence to support Hill's testimony.

The Brock book is damaging in the degree to which it provides names, dates, and details of how far radical right wingers are willing to go in discrediting Democrats in general and liberals in particular. But for our purpose, what is most revealing is not only the extent to which the Christian Right walks lockstep with the political right in this mean-spirited crusade, but the outright hypocrisy that lies behind it. An example is Gil Davis, a failed Virginia politician who is head of the Christian Action Network, a Christian Right group that claims to promote traditional morality and family values. Brock writes of Davis, "In Virginia political circles, the enormously round, jolly lawyer was notorious for womanizing. We hung out together at a reception one evening at the Georgetown Four Seasons Hotel, where Davis was a font of virtually nonstop sexual banter."[5]

Brock's book offers disturbing details of just how low American politics have sunk in recent years. He knows first hand what has happened to Republicans, but we are not naive enough to think similar tales could not be told of Democrats. The reality is that for both major parties ends now justify means to the point where truth hardly matters at all. Opponents are considered enemies to be vanquished. But the complicity of the Christian Right in all of this is what we find appalling. They should be ashamed that such blindness on their part is why Brock could write of the celebration of the Newt Gingrich-led Republican election victory in 1994:

> We had worked our tails off to make tonight happen, to foment our own revolution, and we were getting sloshed in our celebration of our feat. Although we were advancing the rightest of right-wing agendas for the country, in private our values weren't in sync with the Bible Belt fundamentalism that dictated official party ideology. As the evening wound down, I escorted one prominent conservative magazine columnist out the front door after he pushed me onto the bed into a pile of coats and tried to stick his tongue down my throat.[6]

One of the most telling examples of what's wrong with the Christian Right Brock cites is its response when his homosexuality became public. Rather than rejecting him, as he expected, they said virtually nothing, that is, until he disputed the accuracy of a claim made by former FBI agent, Gary Aldrich, in his book, *Unlimited Access*. Alrich wrote that President Clinton had been secretly taken under a blanket to the Marriott Hotel in Washington to have sex with a woman waiting for him there. Brock had been the one who had told Aldrich about the rumor in the first place. Later he told Aldrich he had found absolutely nothing to corroborate it. Undeterred, Aldrich proceeded to put it in his book anyway as an embarrassment to Clinton. Brock's decision not to support Aldrich publicly produced the response from the Christian Right to his being gay he had initially expected. Aldrich, meanwhile, was hailed as "doing the Lord's work—we're glad you were born in America."[7]

It is, of course, entirely possible that *Blinded by the Right* is another Brock ruse in the vein of *The Real Anita Hill*. But he had already begun the split with his neo-conservative friends when he did not engage in character assassination of Hillary

Clinton when he wrote, *The Seduction of Hillary Rodham*. As revealing as the book is about the Christian Right/radical Republican collusion, it is even more telling in its details of Brock's own hypocrisy. That he chose not to vilify Hillary Clinton with unsubstantiated charges as he had done to Anita Hill, coupled with his conservative base rejecting the book for this reason, suggests that Brock might indeed have gone through a genuine crisis of conscience. At the very least, the Brock book has not been challenged on the basis of the facts it presents, and stands as a confirmation of the political agenda the Christian Right passes off as "the Christian way" and the hypocrisy of that claim. Worse, this way of behaving seems to be quite intentional, as a Christian Right internal squabble last year revealed.

Representative Gil Gutknecht (R-MN), a Christian Right Congressman, came under attack from his Christian Right supporters for a bill he sponsored that would allow individual Americans to buy FDA-approved drugs from other countries at lower prices. A California Christian Right organization named Traditional Values Coalition (TVC) claimed the Gutknecht bill "would open the floodgates for RU-486 [abortion pill] and other harmful drugs." Other Christian Right groups joined the fight, including Jerry Falwell. A spokesman for the American Conservative Union that has always supported Gutknecht called the bill "socialistic" and a "liberal scheme." Falwell began to rally his troops against the bill. "Once these drugs hit the American drug supply," he preached, "there is no controlling where they go and whom they impact."

Gutknecht's reaction was swift and candid, suggesting Falwell was suffering from "extreme paranoia." Further, he said, "In this business, the only currency that you carry with you is credibility. And I think the pro-life groups and Jerry Falwell and some of the research groups that have bit on this have lost an enormous amount of credibility."

He's singing our song, of course, especially when he says, "If you say something that's not true, that's a lie. And so they are lying."[8] We couldn't have said it better ourselves. Lying is a primary reason the Christian Right is plagued with the problem of hypocrisy. The most that can be said in their defense is that they are prone to "leaping before looking." But the preponderance of evidence suggests something much more disturbing. They show not the slightest hesitation in making statements they would be hard pressed to show they did not know were untrue.[8]

Jesus once said that people would be known by their fruits (Matthew 7:20). The Christian Right would do well to remember that hypocrisy is a spoiled fruit indeed.

10

ENOUGH OF HISTORICAL REVISIONISM

In the *60 Minutes* interview Falwell claimed he had read the history of the Prophet Muhammad, its founder, written by Muslims and non-Muslims, all of which had convinced him that the Prophet was a terrorist. Though he did not have the opportunity to go beyond these statements on *60 Minutes*, based on his many public statements about Islam and Muslims, it is a safe assumption that Falwell and his Christian Right believe Islam had a violent birth and has lived by violence ever since. That one could say precisely the same thing about Judaism and Christianity aside, Falwell and the Christian Right have shown again that they seldom let historical facts get in the way of their opinions.

Muhammad did engage in violence, of that there is no dispute, but a thorough knowledge of the context reveals that it was a result of conflict with the culture hostile to his efforts to establish Islam. More than anything else, his violence was a matter of self-defense. Born in 570 C. E., Muhammad was forty years old when he began receiving what he believed were revelations of the one true religion of Allah. Illiterate his entire life, his revelations continued for twenty-three years and were written down by his followers into what today is the Qu'ran. Under intense persecution by non-believers for teaching his revelations, in 622 Muhammad and his followers left the city of Mecca and traveled to Medina. This migration now marks the beginning of the Muslim calendar. Years later Muhammad and his followers returned to Mecca, where it is said they forgave their enemies. What we do know as fact is that from that point Islam began a rapid expansion that was peaceful.

Yet it is also true that the perception of Islam as a faith that endorses terrorism is more than a caricature based on the acts of Muslim extremists such as the ones who flew into the Pentagon and World Trade Center. Passages within the Qu'ran itself are sufficiently ambiguous to lend themselves to be used by extremists to support their actions. But the Christian Right ignores the fact that this is also the case with the "sacred texts" of Christianity and Judaism. The writings and interpretations within each of the Abrahamic faiths contain "violence of God" verses that allow radicals to justify their bigoted attitudes and acts of violence. Jack Nelson-Pallmeyer, author of *Is Religion Killing Us?* to which we have already made reference, issues a compelling challenge to all three faith tradition, especially Islam and Christianity, to confront this element of tyranny in their primary texts. Moreover, only a cursory knowledge of history is needed to understand that Christian violence through the centuries may have no religious parallels. The list of atrocities is too long for our purposes, but the words of Martin Luther can serve as a summary of centuries of Christian persecution of Jews and Muslims.

> What then shall we Christians do with this damned, rejected race of Jews? First, their synagogues or churches should be set on fire…Secondly, their homes should likewise be broken down and destroyed…They ought to be put under one roof or in a stable, like Gypsies. Fourthly, their rabbis must be forbidden under threat of death to teach any more…Fifthly, passport and traveling privileges should be absolutely forbidden to the Jews…Sixthly, they ought to be stopped from usury. All their cash and valuables of silver and gold ought to be taken from them and put aside for safe keeping…Seventhly, let the young and strong Jews and

Jewesses be given the flail, the axe, the hoe, the spade,
the distaff, and spindle and let them earn their bread
by the sweat of their noses as is enjoined upon Adam's
children…

To sum up, dear princes and nobles who have Jews
in your domains, if this advice of mine does not suit
you, then find a better one so that you and we may all
be free of this insufferable devilish burden—the Jews.[1]

Quoting Luther is not intended to single out the Reformer
for his anti-Semitism. The sad truth is that he stood in a long
line of Christian clergy and secular leaders who hated the Jews
and did everything in their power to convert and/or kill them.
The Crusades of the eleventh century also subjected Muslims
to the same treatment in the name of Christ. In light of this
history, it is hardly credible for the Christian Right to claim
that Islam is a religion that advocates violence. Misguided zeal
always leads to religion being used in evil ways. And that is
the point. The Christian Right wants to ignore this fact of
Christian history, but it is not much of an exaggeration to say
that this history suggests that with Christians as friends, God
doesn't need any enemies.

Perhaps the Christian Right could show it is humbled by the
disturbing record of Christian persecution by speaking out
against the misrepresentation of the Qu'ran's teaching on the
meaning of "jihad." Though dictionaries define the word as "holy
war," its literal meaning in the Qu'ran is simply "effort." Radical
Muslims argue that verses such as, "So obey not the disbelievers,
but make a great jihad [effort] against them [by preaching] with
it [the Qu'ran]" (Surah 25:52) justify violent "efforts" against
unbelievers who they believe work against the will of Allah. In
doing so they ignore other passages in the Qu'ran such as "The
best jihad is [by] the one who strives against his own self for
Allah, The Mighty and Majestic" (Surah 4:95). It is this inward
"jihad" that most Muslims believe prepares one to make effort
against others, but it is true that the Qu'ran does not state
unequivocally that such violence would be inconsistent with
one's inward need for purification.

All Christians, especially the Christian Right, need to respect
that Muslims read the Qu'ran in different ways, much the way

we read the Christian Bible. Islam is also much more diverse and dynamic than most Christians suppose. One writer puts it:

> Islam, which counts 1 billion adherents and is in nearly every country around the globe, is not monolithic but rather a "tradition-in-the-making," in the words of Omid Safi, professor of Islam at Colgate University. There are Muslim feminists, fundamentalists, democratic reformers, mystics, conservatives, liberals, and so on. As a tradition-in-the-making, Islam is undergoing change and transformation, no small part of it coming from Muslims living in the West who are challenging more conservative views of some of their core-religionists.[2]

Not only is Islam diverse, it shows amazing respect for the Christian Jesus, something about which the Christian Right also seems unaware. Taken together, first within the Qu'ran and subsequently in numerous other Islamic literary traditions, Islamic writings form the largest non-Christian corpus of material relating to Jesus in the world, so much so that it has been referred to as the "Muslim gospel."[3] Much of the knowledge of the educated within pre-modern Islam about Jesus came from this material rather than the Bible.[4] And what does this material say? "In its totality, this gospel is the story of a love affair between Islam and Jesus and is thus a unique record of how one world religion chose to adopt the central figure of another, coming to recognize him as constitutive of its own identity."[5]

At the same time, the tensions between Christians and Muslims center on Jesus, not only in terms of who he was, but in his attitude toward his own followers. The Qu'ran teaches that next to Mohammed, Jesus was God's most revered prophet, including all the prophets of Israel. But it rejects claims that he was divine, which it says is a misrepresentation by Jesus' followers of who he truly was. The Qu'ran was from the beginning "primarily concerned with rectifying a certain doctrinal image of Jesus through its portrayal of Jesus and had little to say on his ministry, teachings, and passion."[6] Consequently, the Muslim gospel, that is, the non-Qu'ranic material about Jesus, probably arose to fill the void about his life[7] —but not so as to contradict the Qu'ranic view of Jesus as a man who did God's will and has a special place in God's realm because of it, not because he was somehow God in the flesh.

What is curious is that this dispute between Christians and Muslims over the "real" Jesus is not so different from the theological conflicts within Christianity before and after the creedal declarations of the church, the ones having to do with the nature of Jesus, whether he was human, divine, or both.[8] In addition, the tensions between the two faiths have been exacerbated by the claim of final "truth" each makes for its sacred writings. Muslims argue for the authority of the Qu'ran in the same way that Christians do for the Bible, asserting that in Qu'ranic texts one can sense "God's power over what is being narrated." Thus, "[God] knows then, and He knows now, how the human story will end, since He is, as it were, the creator-narrator of history. It follows that what is being narrated is the 'best' and the most 'truthful' of all narratives: the final version."[9]

The bottom line to which all of this leads is that there are millions of Muslims and Christians who do not understand what each believes about its own faith or what each understands about the other. But what is not difficult for either to do is to admit that neither is innocent of extremists in their respective traditions acting in violent ways that contradict its central message. This is why we wonder if it wasn't intentional that the Christian Right ignored the immediate renunciations of the acts of 9/11 from the most respected of Muslims leaders, as well as the expressions of sympathy for the American people they offered. An example was one from Shaikh Abdul-Azeez Aal ash-Shaikh, the Grand Mufti and the Chief Justice of the Supreme Judiciary Council of Saudi Arabia, who wrote:

> Based upon what has preceded, it is obligatory for all of us to know—both states and societies, Muslims and Non-Muslims—a number of important matters:
> 1. That these matters that have taken place in the United States and whatever else is of their nature of plane hijackings and taking people hostage or killing

innocent people, without a just cause, this is nothing but a manifestation of injustice, oppression and tyranny, which the Islamic Shari'ah does not sanction or accept, rather it is expressly forbidden and it is amongst the greatest of sins.

2. That the Muslim who learns the details of his religion, and who acts upon the Book of Allah and the Sunnah of His Prophet...does not allow himself to fall into the likes of these actions, due to what they contain of exposing oneself to the wrath of Allah, and then what results from them of harms and corruption (upon the earth).

3. It is obligatory upon the Scholars of the Muslim Ummah that they explain the truth concerning the likes of these affairs (i.e. terrorist attacks) and that they make clear to the world at large that the Shari'ah of Allaah and the religion of Islam does not sanction these types of actions, ever.[10]

Renowned Muslim scholar Sheikh Yusuf al-Qaradawi issued the following statement: "Our hearts bleed for the attacks that have targeted the World Trade Center [WTC], as well as other institutions in the United States despite our strong oppositions to the American biased policy towards Israel on the military, political and economic fronts."[11]

The attitude of the Christian Right toward Islam ignores that interpreters of a faith tradition not their own must always yield to "insider" interpreters. This is the only reliable way to gain a balanced understanding of that tradition's sacred writings. The Christian Right would surely argue, for example, that a Muslim's interpretation of the Bible must yield to theirs simply because they are Muslim and not Christian. Yet they fail to offer the same courtesy to Muslim interpreters of the Qu'ran.

Also, some "political" fundamentalists join the Christian Right in refusing to learn from history. Paul Weyrich recently wrote of Islam:

Give credit to the Council on American Islamic Relations, the American Muslim Council and other members of the American Muslim disinformation lobby for using generous donations from foreign lands to package a sanitized version of Islam as peaceful and tolerant. But their fantasy Islam collides with the truth about life inside those countries where the religion is dominant. Unfortunately, too many Americans are willing to believe that Islam is a gentle lamb of a religion, rather than the lion with blood on its claws, ready to pounce once more on unsuspecting innocents—and that it is being prodded to do so by its most devout believers.

This does not mean that all Muslims are that way. But all it takes is a small minority who take its scriptures (which Muslims consider to be words dictated by Allah himself) literally to destroy the peace of the nation and the world at large.[12]

His point is well taken, except that this is precisely what we believe he and the Christian Right represent—a minority who take both Hebrew and Christian scriptures literally to destroy the peace of the nation and the world at large. It is an enigma that it does not matter to Weyrich that Judaism has been the primary object of Christian hatred, that Hitler's effort to exterminate Jews was not at all inconsistent with Christian efforts to expel them from most of Europe. Nor was Hitler's requirement that they wear the Star of David unlike The Fourth Lateran Council's decree that Jews and Muslims were to wear special dress, or the Synod of Narbonne's degree that Jews wear oval badges. Though Weyrich speaks as if none of this history matters, liberal Christian cannot. We will not be part of a modern-day effort to advance a Christian triumphalism that is a reminder of past evils and justifies religious wars today. We choose to raise our voices in a chorus of protest to this kind of historical ignorance.

The Christian Right claims to speak truth. Yet the truth it wants to deny is that Christians have no moral basis for speaking about the judgment of God on anyone. None. At best we might hope that God truly is gracious and forgiving and that the sins of our past we seem determined to perpetuate today will not cause us to be left outside divine mercy, should a day of reckoning actually come. If any group should worry about the Great Day of Judgment, history would suggest it should be Christians.

At the same time, not one of the three great monotheistic faiths has any right to claim moral superiority over the others. In her book, *The Battle for God*,[13] Karen Armstrong provides a detailed history of the rise of fundamentalism within Judaism, Christianity, and Islam. How ironic that each has always had friends that have made enemies unnecessary. All three have suffered under the impact of radical fringe groups within them. We believe the Christian Right is the source of this problem within Christianity. In warning of the dangers radical Muslim states pose to America, and, thus, to Christianity, they are naming the demon that lies within themselves.

This is why Charles Kimball's book, *When Religion Becomes Evil*, is important. He names five warning signs of religion becoming a force for evil. Each underscores the dangers religious zealots in all faith traditions pose. They are: (1) Absolute Truth Claims; (2) Blind Obedience; (3) Establishing the "Ideal" Time; (4) The End Justifies The Means; (5) Declaring Holy War.[14] Kimball's examples of the ways these signs manifest themselves among Christians are telling indictments of the Christian Right, though he does not name them directly.

As common as these signs are, every religion thinks it is the one not guilty of manifesting them. The Christian Right acts as if these constitute what being a Christian means. They eschew any notion that there is no absolute truth. They are quite sure they have it because the Bible (they say) says Jesus is the only way. Obedience is "blind" only if you are not a Christian. But if you are, obedience is expected in order to stand up for the absolute truth of which you alone are in possession. You also know Jesus is coming soon. Although you may not know the hour, you know it is "soon" because all the "signs" point to it, fueling evangelistic zeal to convert others. To that end any means are employed because the end for those who do not respond to your message is doom. One of the clear signs of the imminent return of Jesus is the "war" those following false gods are waging against Christ's elect. The battle is between good and evil, Christians and non-Christians.

Anyone who doesn't support this holy war, though the Christian Right seldom calls it this openly, is naive about evil or has given in to liberal relativism.

It is easy to understand why the Christian Right can ignore Kimball's five signs of religion becoming evil, but the rest of the nation cannot. Liberal Christians must not think these people will go away or that the long-term effect of their religious zeal will be minimal. History cries out to us not to be dismissive or naive about what people will do in the name of God. The Christian Right is dangerous and powerful. How ironic that they actually believe they are being persecuted. The reasons they do and the absurdity of such a claim is the topic to which we now turn our attention.

11

ENOUGH OF THE PERSECUTION COMPLEX

According to the Christian Right, Christianity in America is being persecuted by godless liberals.

> While Jesus said to expect persecution if we live for Him, that doesn't absolve the persecutors from responsibility for their hypocritical actions, especially when they claim to be the champions of tolerance, diversity, pluralism, and academic freedom.

This statement by Cal Thomas, Christian Right columnist, appears on the back cover of David Limbaugh's book, *Persecution: How Liberals Are Waging War Against Christianity*. The book is praised by Christian Right public figures for exposing the ways Christians are under attack by liberals who rule schools, businesses, the courts, and the public square. "With passion and precision," writes Michele Malkin, another radical Right columnist, "David Limbaugh provides overwhelming evidence of discrimination against Christians in America." She concludes that the book "exposes the hypocrisy and bigotry of the secular, anti-Christian Left" and serves as "a call to arms for all true believers of religious liberty to reclaim their rightful place in the public square."

D. James Kennedy of Coral Ridge Ministries applauds *Persecution*, convinced that by "documenting" intolerance against Christians, the book is "sorely needed when the only 'acceptable' prejudice of our day is the bias against Christians." Sean Hannity of Fox News endorses the book by claiming that liberals have undermined the Constitution as well as declared war on Americans of faith "who have made America the beacon of freedom and justice that it is."

The idea that Christians in America are victims of persecution is almost laughable, given the fact that from the founding of the nation Christians, especially white males, have enjoyed the privileges of living in this country unencumbered by the discrimination many other individuals and groups have faced. Whatever "persecution" Christians have experienced has come from other Christians, as Quakers and New England Baptists encountered in Colonial America. The Christian Right trying to place themselves in the same category with those who have had to fight and continue to fight for constitutional rights that the Christian Right exercises freely has the feel of the privileged crying foul because some of their perks have been taken away. For the Christian Right there is nothing extreme about this claim in the least, as the statements below from other Christian Righters illustrate. Limbaugh asked them the question, "Why do you suppose that Christians have been singled out for discrimination in American society?"[1] Here are their answers.

> **James Dobson**: Conservative Christians are subjected to such virulent hostility primarily because we pose a threat to the leftist, immoral agenda of the media and entertainment industries. When believers conform to the dictates of scripture, they have the temerity to stand against abortion, euthanasia, "population control," condom distribution, pornography, sexual license, and the tax-and-spend policies of liberal government. Above all else, religious conservatives are hated because some of them—very few, unfortunately—are willing to oppose the gay and lesbian agenda in all its excesses, from the push to legalize same-sex "marriage" and adoption to lowering the age of consent, to the advancement of pro-homosexual school

curriculum, and the construction of "bath house" establishments.[2]

Michael Novak: A small minority of Americans, about six or seven percent, mostly from the highly educated elite, have their reasons for despising Christianity, and they make their hostility quite evident...This elite seems to dominate the national voices of the legal profession (although not, I think, the local voices of the legal profession), a large segment of the movie stars, and a significant number of opinion leaders in the media. Of course, feminists, gays, and the fanatical secularists who gather around People for the American Way and the American Civil Liberties Union (although there are many good people in these organizations too) are directly opposed to traditional Christian belief and practice, and, therefore, to orthodox Catholics and faithful evangelicals.[3]

Marvin Olasky: I don't see Christians as singled out for discrimination in American society generally—after all, big chunks of American society are heavily populated with Christians—but the bias is clear in two sectors of society (academic and media) that in turn influence others.[4]

D. James Kennedy: Well, I think that there's probably pretty general consensus among most knowledgeable people that the one thing that the "tolerant" cannot tolerate is Christianity, which they would like to brand as intolerant. I think that many times people don't realize it, but when you begin to allow every kind of immorality and degeneracy and perversion imaginable, the one thing you will not allow is to have anybody criticize you for doing these things...In addition, when you don't want to obey the Commandments of God, you find it very difficult to acknowledge that these are absolute truths presented by an absolute God that demands absolute obedience when you have determined you are not going to obey and so you must get rid of absolutes to begin with.[5]

The mindsets these statements reveal makes a sense of victimization unavoidable. That Limbaugh acknowledges other groups have experienced discrimination rings hollow when it is made in the context of arguing that Christians face a "different" kind of persecution because society decries mistreatment of other groups, but "when it comes to anti-Christian discrimination, the culture's attitude seems to be, 'Yes, please do shut up those Bible-thumping idiots'."[6] Moreover, he says that the perpetrators of this persecution are "legion," behind every tree ready to leap out and beat up on unsuspecting Christians just because they are Christians.[7]

To begin to understand the argument this book pursues, one needs to remember that Limbaugh is not only Rush's brother, in every sense of the word, he is a lawyer. There is a saying among attorneys that if you cannot convince them with facts, baffle them with BS. Limbaugh executes this strategy to perfection. From beginning to end the book reads like a transcript of a court case in which the prosecuting attorney seeks to overwhelm the jury with a parade of evidence that hides the weakness of his case. What Limbaugh writes obscures truth rather than uncovering it. He makes general claims and then proceeds to cite examples ad nauseum until the sheer volume of "evidence" convinces readers of their veracity. The weaker the argument, the more "evidence" he presents. But in the end what we find is nothing more than the skewed way the Christian Right see themselves and the rest of us. It's not unlike reading so much bad news in the morning paper that you get the feeling the world is going to hell in a hand basket. It may be, but reading bad news does not make the case for it. It simply establishes that bad things happen. Whether or not they outnumber or outweigh the good things is a separate issue.

The first salvo Limbaugh fires is directed at public education. Schools and the teachers and administrators in charge of them have become a microcosm of what the Christian Right believes is wrong with this country. The first case in point Limbaugh cites is a ruling made in May, 1995, by Samuel Kent, U.S. District Judge for the Southern District of Texas, who, according to Limbaugh, "decreed that any student uttering the word 'Jesus' would be arrested and incarcerated for six months."[8]

He then lifts a quote from the ruling to show how nefarious the judge was:

> And make no mistake, the court is going to have a United States marshal in attendance at the graduation. If any student offends this court, that student will be summarily arrested and will face up to sixth months incarceration in the Galveston County Jail for contempt of court...Anyone who thinks I'm kidding about this order better think again...Anyone who violates these orders, no kidding, is going to wish that he or she had died as a child when this court gets through with it.

Notice that Limbaugh claims the court ruling forbids any student from uttering the word "Jesus," as if this was a blanket ruling that would put a student in jail for talking about Jesus to a friend standing next to her locker. But the issue had to do with a high school graduation, as Limbaugh later admits. Not only did the judge forbid references to all deities, not just the God of Christians, he was confronting a school system that had been allowing students to offer Christian prayers at official school functions. In a strange twist of logic, however, Limbaugh says that this fact confirms that the judge's orders intended to target Christians since they were the only ones who had been praying at school functions.[9]

All of this is quite misleading about the judge's order. The net effect of the ruling was that Christians were prohibited from praying at the school's commencement, only because they were the ones who had been doing it and had stated publicly they were going to continue to do so. Had the judge not spoken forcefully about how serious he was and what the consequences would be for ignoring the injunction, Christian prayers at the graduation ceremony would have been offered. Moreover, it is a safe bet that had Muslim prayers been sanctioned by the school system and were being planned for commencement, the Christian Right would have gone to court not in support of their freedom to make their witness, but to forbid them from doing so.

Before readers—or "jurors"—have time to catch their breath, though, Limbaugh launches into other examples of Christian "persecution" to augment the Texas case. It's the way of the entire book. Chapter after chapter of one "horror" story after another illustrating how Christians are subjected to vicious liberal persecution, from public schools to the public square to Hollywood to private enterprise to societal values. His theme is clear: "Every time a student's right to invoke God is denied, often due to overblown concerns about the indirect involvement of the state in religion, we must remember that his speech and religious freedom are being suppressed."[10]

This shows a radicalism that makes the Christian Right's position on church and state relations off center and out of balance. Students and citizens in general can and do invoke God in various and appropriate ways. What they are prohibited from doing is exercising this freedom in a way that is sanctioned by tax–supported institutions or with government approval imposing Christianity on non-Christians.

Let's be clear. It is Christianity that is at the center of this controversy. Not once in the history of this nation have Jews argued for their right to offer prayers in classrooms, hold morning devotions for an entire school, pray at graduation ceremonies, or place the Ten Commandments in courthouses. The Christian Right believes this country was founded upon the Judeo–Christian heritage, so long as the "Christian" part is supreme. What they don't like about school policies is the fact that Christianity's privileged position has been lessened. That is the extent of the "persecution" Christians now suffer. We lost our position of power. Let me share a personal story to illustrate.

In 1961 Raymond Berry, the all-pro wide receiver for the then-Baltimore Colts, came to my high school to speak to a required morning assembly and the annual football awards banquet that evening. At the assembly he began by telling a few humorous stories from his experiences in the NFL, paused, and then proceeded to tell everyone present—Christian and non-Christian—that the real reason he had come to speak to all of us was that he wanted to tell us what Jesus Christ meant to his life. The rest of his talk was a testimony of the before and after of his Christian conversion, ending with a call for those listening who had not already done so to consider making Jesus Christ Lord and Savior of their lives. His speech got mixed reviews, as one might expect, and created what might be considered a mild controversy, but it certainly did not result in action by the school to avoid such an incident again. In fact, the next season Christian ministers once again gave the invocation before the start of the Friday night football games.

This true story points to why the courts stepped in, just as Judge Samuel Kent did in Texas, ruling that government cannot favor one religion over another or favor freedom of religion over freedom *from* religion, as in the 1962 watershed case, *Engel v. Vitale*. According to the Christian Right, this is when God got kicked out of school, i.e., Christian prayers were ruled unconstitutional. Since then the Christian Right has ranted and raved and now wants those on whom it was once free to impose its religious views to believe Christianity is being persecuted. How ironic that we who represent the majority of the American population are being persecuted by such a tiny minority.[11] Of course, the Christian Right argues that the percentage of true Christians is much smaller, the implication being that "liberal" Christians suffer from an unconscious self-hatred to the extent that we are waging war against ourselves.

As ridiculous as that may seem, it is no less so than the way the Christian Right interprets American history. No one disputes the fact that Christianity was the dominant faith when America was founded, and still is. Many of our founders had a vibrant faith, while others did not, but that Christianity influenced their thinking, values, and worldview is not in debate. What is in question is the Christian Right's insistence that our founders intended governments, especially at the state level, to allow Christians to use public venues to do what Limbaugh says is endemic to their faith—evangelize. What he and other Christian Righters fail to see is that the heart of democracy requires the protection of the minority against the tyranny of the majority. This is why the Establishment Clause of the Constitution contains a two-fold prohibition on the government. It cannot establish a religion and it cannot prohibit the free exercise thereof. Of course Christian prayers in schools, personal testimonies at graduation, and Christian displays in courthouses violate the first part of the Establishment Clause. If the courts allowed government officials at any level to sponsor or sanction such Christian acts, it would force those same officials into the role of ensuring the right of all religions to have the same opportunity. In short order the relationship between church and state would become so entangled chaos would rule, and the Christian Right whose children would be forced to listen to prayers and testimonies of other religions, would be the first to protest.

Some of the examples in *Persecution* show actual excesses by school officials who have erred on the side of caution when deciding how to stay within the boundaries of court rulings. But without exception they have been corrected when challenged. The record shows that court decisions by liberal and conservative judges have been amazingly consistent in deciding where the line is between church and state. The truth is, no court can satisfy the Christian Right except to allow them complete freedom to use their own discretion about what they will and will not do in all aspects of American society. Limbaugh even faults the conservative Rehnquist Court, though not the Chief Justice himself, for adding "further restrictions on school prayer" by barring Christian ministers from praying at official graduation ceremonies.[12] Not even free speech guidelines contained in the current administration's "No Child Left Behind Act" are enough. As referenced by Limbaugh, those regulations specifically say that students can read Bibles, say grace before meals, and study religious materials during non-instructional hours.[13]

Limbaugh and the Christian Right believe America is "the greatest, freest nation in the history of the world."[14] Why the greatest? Isn't being a great nation sufficient? Not if you believe this nation was founded by Christians on Christian beliefs and principles, and Christianity is the greatest religion in the history of the world. If America were not the greatest nation, it would, according to their logic, raise questions about the supremacy of Christianity. The God of Christians could not possibly be the titular head of a nation that was inferior to another, especially if that other nation were not Christian. This is also why the Christian Right supports American militarism. Might makes right!

A major fault in Christian Right thinking is the fact that they pay no attention either to the past record of how Christian Americans (not American Christians) have exercised their hegemony or the danger inherent in all religions, including Christianity. They think it is nothing more than liberal hype. As far as Limbaugh is concerned, non-Christians should welcome an unfettered exercise of religious devotion by the Christian Right. Some may blanch at the mere suggestion that our freedom could have originated from Christian-based principles, Limbaugh says, because they view Christianity as an authoritarian, inflexible religion antithetical to liberty. They think of Christianity as synonymous with intolerance and rigidity, and incompatible with freedom of choice. Some harbor the irrational fear that Christians want to establish a theocratic Christian state. That could be one reason, he surmises, that they are afraid to allow the facts of history to speak for themselves. Ironically, he concludes, if secularists would open themselves up to America's historical record, their fears would be allayed, as they would come to understand that Christianity undergirds, rather than undermines, our freedom. Instead, Christian precepts formed the intellectual underpinnings of American constitutional government.[15]

This is the kind of revisionist history of which Limbaugh accuses liberals.[16] When the Declaration of Independence and the U.S. Constitution were conceived, written, and ratified, our founders understood that all the freedoms of which they spoke were for white males, women to a lesser degree, and blacks not all. That Christianity was the major influence on them, therefore, is more indictment than endorsement. For Christians to accept women being treated as second-class citizens and black Americans as animals scandalizes the gospel rather than promoting it. Worse, these kinds of perversions of the Christian gospel continue to plague us. Yet the Christian Right wants to take down the "wall" of separation between church and state that exists because of them, in the name of Christianity always protecting the freedoms of everyone.

It is sad but true that history shows clearly that non-Christians have reason to worry when Christians like the Christian Right are in charge. It is endemic of narrow-minded faith to engage in discrimination, and if need be, outright persecution. Not only does the past make this clear, but so does the present. Consider these two examples:

The Southern Baptist Convention is the largest of all Protestant denominations in America. It is also undergoing a brutal schism that has caused personal pain and agony at all levels of the SBC. This split has one cause, and only one. Fundamentalists within the Convention have systematically "purged" the Foreign Mission Board, every association office where possible, and its major seminaries. The "purging" of "liberal" faculty was especially vicious at Southern Baptist Theological Seminary in Louisville, Kentucky, Midwestern Baptist Seminary in Kansas City, Missouri, and Southeastern Baptist Theological Seminary in Wake Forest, North Carolina. Respected pastors, educators, and denominational leaders were labeled heretics and their faith disparaged by those leading this takeover. As a consequence, and in spite of the hostility to which they have been subjected, those pushed out formed the Cooperative Baptist Fellowship. They have maintained ties with the SBC through support for the Foreign Mission Board's work, working together to embody the spirit of unity and tolerance for diversity that once characterized Southern Baptist life.

If that were not enough, the Missouri Synod Lutheran Church sought to defrock the Rev. David Benke for his participation in a service of worship held at Yankee Stadium two days after 9/11 because non-Christians also participated in the service. Rev. Benke was the object of hate mail and malicious attacks on his faith. In his own words:

> The very next day, I began to get messages filled with hate. They were messages not from people outside of my tradition, but from within my tradition. And they were messages that nailed me to the floor, frankly, emotionally. They just said, "You were wrong to be there. You never should have gone to Yankee Stadium. You are a heretic.

You have dishonored your faith." One man said genuine terrorism was me. He said, planes crash and people die, nothing big about that. Genuine terrorism was me giving that prayer. I just want to say that I have not gotten over that and I can't get through that. Because I lived through the real terrorists driving the planes into the real buildings. And I've talked to people whose loved ones were murdered. And for me to be put in that same category is just not tolerable to me. I can't take it. I can't bear up under it. It doesn't make any sense to me. Within two months, a number of those people put together a petition and filed charges of heresy, saying that I am not part of the Christian Church because of what I did on that day and should not be part of my denomination anymore, should not be allowed to preach, should have my collar removed.[17]

Thankfully, Rev. Benke recently regained his standing after a two-year ordeal to defend himself against the kind of religious intolerance the Christian Right promotes in the name of freedom of religion.

This kind of extremism points to why the claim of Christians being persecuted falls so flat. Those who "persecute" others in the name of religious purity have no moral grounds for claiming they are victims of the same treatment.

12

ENOUGH OF THE WRONG ISSUES

The first thing that is "really" wrong with the Christian Right is they create barriers between people rather than building bridges. The truth is, the Christian Right has little appeal among non-Christians. Their voice is heard the same way we hear it: judgmental, self-righteous, narrow-minded, prejudicial, moralistic. Issues are too complicated for simplistic solutions, and the world is too volatile to label people who oppose your views as enemies.

The second thing that is "really" wrong with the Christian Right is its agenda, and liberal Christians are the living proof. You see, the Christian Right believes liberals are the reason for the moral decline of the nation. But many of us grew up with daily prayer and the Pledge of Allegiance as part of our public school routine, two bedrock issues the Christian Right says can turn this country around. If that is the case, how is it that liberals who grew up with both have led the country to the abyss? Either their agenda or their logic is faulty.

But these two "wrongs" only scratch the surface of what's wrong with the Christian Right. They seem obsessed with sex, whether it is homosexuality, sex education in schools, internet porn, or Hollywood films. Sex is the heart and soul of their moral preaching. Not that sex isn't a major player in human behavior. We simply believe it is shortsighted to limit moral concerns to sex. We believe matters of social justice are as important to a nation's moral fiber as sexual behavior. The Christian Right's record on such issues, however, underscores the fact that they disagree.

They vilified Bill Clinton during the Monica Lewinsky scandal, with liberal Christian leaders also very critical of his actions. Yet the Christian Right was silent about the sexual misconduct of then Speaker of the House, Newt Gingrich, his designated successor, Bob Livingston, and Rep. Henry Hyde who chaired the impeachment committee in the House. The Christian Right wants to be the moral police for the nation, yet exempts Republican politicians from their righteous indignation. But woe to any liberal who gets caught with "his" pants down, and a free pass to any Republicans who do.

The Christian Right can preach against sins of the flesh with passion, but their words will have little authenticity to us until they stop playing partisan politics and begin bringing the power of their public voice to issues of social justice. It is easy to focus on "sexy" issues while ignoring the weightier matters of the law. In the words of Jesus himself,

> Woe to you, scribes and Pharisees, hypocrites! For you tithe mint, dill, and cumin, and have neglected the weightier matters of the law: justice and mercy and faith. It is these you ought to have practiced without neglecting the others. You blind guides! You strain at a gnat but swallow a camel! (Matthew 23:23)

We do not believe Christian Righters are blind guides, but they certainly seem to wear blinders and spend a lot of time straining at gnats. We suggest they begin to devote attention to the bigger picture. Below are some of the issues liberal Christians believe fill in that larger picture. The first ones relate directly to the question of the relationship of faith and politics, while the others reflect more general concerns.

Corporate Greed and Freedom of the Press

The Christian Right never tires of singing the blues about the "liberal press" skewing the news with its ideological bias, even though evidence points to the contrary.[1] The Christian Right is correct in being concerned about accurate news, but wrong when it comes to seeing the real threat. Liberals are not the problem when it comes to the press. Giant media conglomerates are. They are a threat not only to the Christian Right, but to liberal Christians, and everyone who cares about fair and accurate news reporting. Journalists Bill Moyers and William Safire, despite having contrasting political perspectives, have been leading voices sounding the alarm about this threat. In strong language and in more than a few of his *New York Times* columns, Safire criticized the 2003 FCC decision to allow an expansion of media control into the hands of a few giant corporations, wondering aloud why his media colleagues had not understood what was at stake. Moyers has devoted several segments of his PBS show, *NOW*, to this issue. In a November 28, 2003 broadcast in particular, he said that he is often asked why, as a journalist, he keeps coming back to the story of media and democracy. His answer bears repeating.

He began by recounting a story he was told by Jim Bouton, former pitching star for the New York Yankees. Bouton is as well known in literary circles as he is among baseball fans because of his 1970 book, *Ball Four*. The book was a candid account of the adolescent behavior of professional players driven by overstuffed hormones spending as much time socializing as getting ready to play ball. Moyers noted that the New York Public Library recently chose *Ball Four* as one of the 100 "Books of the Century." But it is Bouton's more recent book, *Foul Ball*, that drew Moyers's attention on *NOW*. Moyers has noted that the story Bouton tells has been disputed by the newspaper involved, but thus far the essential details have not been proven erroneous.[2]

It seems the newspaper in Pittsfield, Massachusetts, near where Bouton now lives had urged the public to support the building of a new baseball stadium to the tune of $18.5 million on polluted property the paper owned, a fact the paper failed to disclose. Further, the Pittsfield newspaper is owned by MediaNews Group, based in Denver, which owns 100 "media properties" such as *The Salt Lake Tribune* and *The Denver Post*. When Bouton went to the newspaper publisher with a proposal to renovate the existing historic stadium without using public funds, he was told he would have to discuss it with Dean Singleton who runs MediaNews. Bouton and a colleague tried, but Singleton never returned their calls, even after Bouton sent him a signed copy of *Ball Four*. The reason, of course, was that Singleton's company, along with the largest law firm in Pittsfield, wanted to own the stadium on its own property but with taxpayers footing the bill, something already voted down three times.

The point here, among many, is that free access to important information related to public issues was denied because of vested interests in the outcome by the conglomerate that controls the media. But that is not the end of the story. It seems that the General Electric Corporation is also invested in the media conglomerate involved here. After Bouton's publisher received a call from somebody close to GE, it decided not to publish *Foul Ball* after all, even though they had given him an advance based on the success of his earlier book. They did say he could keep half of it if he remained silent about the whole affair. He refused and published the book himself.

The entire matter is quite disturbing. The ethical violations involved represent a practice that has become all too common today among American corporate executives. This is an alarming tale of what can happen when a city has only one daily paper that refuses to tell the public the truth about politicians and corporate executives getting in bed together while the public pays for the room. Moyers notes that two-thirds of the newspaper markets in America are monopolies. As liberal Christians, we believe this is one of the most serious threats we face in this country. It is an issue of epic proportions because it is driven by greed that is tearing at the moral fabric of our society. Media executives are not driven by a desire to limit people's freedom. They are consumed with making money, and if freedom of the press has to be sacrificed in this pursuit, so be it. As Moyer concluded in his NOW commentary:

> So, yes, I keep coming back to the subject of media conglomeration because it can take the oxygen out of democracy. The founders of this country believed a free and rambunctious press was essential to the protection

of our freedoms. They couldn't envision the rise of giant megamedia conglomerates whose interests converge with state power to produce a conspiracy against the people. I think they would be aghast at how this union of media and government has produced the very kind of imperial power against which they rebelled. So, yes, media conglomeration has become a beat for my colleagues and me. We think this is the most important story of all, the one that determines what other stories get told—and how.

If the Christian Right wants to focus on something that poses a genuine threat to the American way of life, they can join us in supporting the work of people like Bill Moyers and Jim Bouton who are fighting on behalf of all of us. More than that, though, the Christian Right can use their influence to call for an ethical cleansing of corporate America. The last few years have seen one scandal after another in which ordinary people have been cheated out of investments and retirement savings by greedy and unscrupulous executives. The emerging mutual funds crisis is but another example with the potential of reeking more havoc on the pensions of millions of Americans. There is something rotten in corporate America that political window dressing will not fix. If America is experiencing moral decay, the real battlefront is not prayer in public schools but the greed and corruption common place in corporate America. Especially when it threatens the foundation upon which our democracy was founded, freedom of the press.

Truth in Government

Bill Clinton and George W. Bush have more in common than being presidents of the United States. In his own way, each has proven that "doublespeak" is not just the fantasy of an Orwellian future. The now infamous question about the meaning of "is" that Clinton used to hide his deception about the sordid affair with a White House intern brought shame to himself, his family, and America. One wonders how a man as intellectually gifted as he could possibly think it would work to try to use double-speak to cloud the truth about his disgusting behavior. But the answer is obvious. It was a problem of character. He not only behaved in a way that disrespected his office, he couldn't tell the truth about it after he had been exposed.

The same holds true for George W. Bush, only his use of "doublespeak" comes in the form of the truth about his payback of campaign debts. The policy that raised the level of allowable sulfur emissions released by coal-firing power plants was labeled the "Clear Sky Initiative." The much publicized "No Child Left Behind" program was itself left behind when Bush cut its budget in the first year. Tax cuts for the wealthiest Americans were promoted as "aid to the neediest," except that those in the lowest income brackets do not make enough money to pay taxes.

More is going on in these examples than politicians trying to save their own skin or promoting policies by a different name. There is an intentional deceit involved that betrays honesty and integrity in government. It's been around a long time. When civilian casualties of war were first labeled "collateral damage," "double-speak" became a way of life for government cover-ups. But the real casualty was truth. Today it is standard fare for politicians and government agencies to cover up the truth of their actions with words that veil rather than reveal their true intentions.

Instead of the Christian Right waving the American flag in its sanctuaries, we believe a more biblical approach is a position of what we call "critical patriotism" that is ready to support politicians of integrity and government actions grounded in truth and justice, but is also just as ready to expose unethical and dishonest actions by individuals and government, even when those involved are people we have supported for office. The United States is a great nation, but our government often tells lies to cover things it does not want the public to know. We do not serve the people's best interests as Christians to ignore it when it happens.

Corporate Corruption

The news of Enron executives fraudulently banking millions of dollars while the company was going under opened corporate America's Pandora's Box. Writing about the unending revelations about corporate misconduct, columnist Molly Ivins noted that Allan Sloan of *Newsweek* says these are not a case of "a few bad apples." He describes it as an example of "the Cockroach Theory." You see one, and you know there's a whole nest of the nasty maggots.[3] Ivins also quotes Jack A. Blum, a Washington lawyer and expert in money-laundering and other forms of tax evasion:

> Corporate managers have spent the last century developing tools for avoiding regulation and taxation. They brag that acts of tax avoidance are part of corporate productivity. For them, each dollar of tax not paid because of their machinations is the added value they bring to a company. Tax avoidance is a profit center. Avoidance of regulation and supervision is an equally high priority. Corporate contributions and the personal contributions of senior corporate managers have funded anti-regulatory think tanks and anti-regulatory scholarship. Political contributions have turned theory into reality.[4]

This is a serious issue with consequences being felt now and for years to come. But its designed subtlety fails to capture attention in the way it should. Corporate greed, fraud, and mismanagement are offenses against this entire nation. Workers and investors put more than their money in the people who lead these companies. They put their trust in them. It is an egregious violation of the public trust for leaders to behave as many of them do, not to mention the damage they are doing to the financial stability of the nation's economy. Nothing shows the moral decay of the nation more than what is going on in corporate America today.

Yet, unless sex is involved, such as the Abercrombie & Fitch 2003 Christmas catalogue with partially nude models intended to appeal to teenager shoppers, the Christian Right remains shockingly silent about Enron, MCI, Smith/Barney, the emerging Mutual Bonds scandal, and all the other examples of illegal and unethical corporate conduct. That sex is used to entice our young people to more materialism is a serious problem. But it is greed ˙breed by materialism that truly threatens the moral foundations of the nation.

Racism

Our greatest failure as a nation remains our inability to deal with racism and poverty. (Henry Hampton, Executive Director for the War on Poverty)[5]

In 1967 Jerry Falwell founded his Lynchburg Christian Academy as a segregated alternative to the integration of the city's public schools. He now claims this was not the case,[6] but his attempt to rewrite history is exposed by a statement issued by the city's clergy association sharply criticizing the school's racial segregation: "We, sensitive to our Lord's inclusion and to non-whites in our community, deplore the use of the term 'Christian' in connection with the private schools which exclude Negroes and other non-whites." The statement also commended the city's school board for its leadership and creative approaches to sound education, especially the board's integration plan that had been implemented without incident.[7]

Today Falwell says his segregated school was necessary because "Bible reading and prayer had been banned in our public schools." All he was doing was providing children with "moral training and Christian values."[8] Though past racism might be forgiven, its present manifestations do not seem to constitute an issue about which Falwell and the Christian Right seem all that concerned. They think the racial playing field has now been leveled and all minority persons need to do is to trust corporate America, political leaders, school officials, judges, prosecutors, police, government bureaucrats, and other persons in authority—the vast majority of whom are white—to treat them fairly. They think the problem today is reverse discrimination. Minorities want special treatment that necessitates discrimination against whites.

To make this kind of argument is truly a moral stretch. The reality of life in America today is that minorities continue to face brutal racism, ever how subtle it may appear. Only one in our group[9] is black, though several are women and know something about discrimination in their own experience, even in the church. But none of us who is white ever thinks about being watched by security personnel when we go shopping. None of us worries about being pulled over by police for racial profiling. None of us worries about being discriminated against for the color of our skin when we seek employment. None of us encounters fear in the eyes of women or older persons because we are a minority person. Yet all of these are daily experiences for minorities in this country, most especially for black Americans.

A state of Minnesota study released in 2003 confirmed that police stop and search blacks, Latinos, and American Indians at a rate much higher than whites. Examining nearly 200,000 traffic stops made the previous year, the study revealed a "strong likelihood" of racial bias in police policies and practices. Moreover, because no dispatcher cross checks were made on information provided by officers themselves, the study's authors suggested the problem was probably underestimated in the report. Ironically, while minorities were stopped and searched more often, they were less likely to be found with anything illegal.[10]

Reports such as this show how misguided the idea is that minorities need to acknowledge that the racial playing field has been leveled. Indeed, there is nothing so pathetic as hearing a white male complain about minorities getting special treatment when he has lived his entire life with such a benefit. Perhaps affirmative action has been the reason some persons have been passed over in job applications and school admissions. We are not naive enough to believe that every lawsuit brought to court for discrimination has merit. But we also know that when the entire spectrum of today's racial climate is considered, these instances pale in comparison to the discrimination minority persons continue to face.

How could the white majority in this nation ever know the number of times they get jobs over minority applicants because of race? How could we measure the suspicion and even hatred toward minorities in the minds of people in positions of authority? How could we know what it feels like to have to think about the fact that you are a minority person every day of your life? Every time racial profiling leads to police brutality, politicians tell us it will not be tolerated. Every time an employee wins a case against blatant racial discrimination in the work place, corporate leaders tell us procedures have been changed. Every time a church search committee discriminates against minority applicants, clergy become angry. Yet what is lost on most people is the impact this has on minority persons. They don't forget racism exists. They get up every morning living with it, yet not one white person ever has to think about it for themselves.

This is the real world of race relations in this country. To spend energy fighting for prayer in schools or the Pledge of Allegiance while ignoring this issue is moral shortsightedness. To believe that gay and lesbian rights threaten the nation's moral foundations while racism runs rampant is a clear case of straining at a gnat and swallowing a camel. It is very troubling and revealing that not once during the entire time this book has been in process has any Christian Right web site carried an article or even a news story about racism.[11]

Many mainline Christian denominations, on the other hand, beleaguered as they are, spend time and resources dealing with this unacceptable blight on human relations. Three years ago one denomination initiated a major emphasis on racism. Hundreds of workshops across the country have been held and thousands of dollars have been spent educating Christians about its continuing impact. Liberal Christians know that at bottom racism is a matter of the heart and not just law. But we also know that much can be done to make white America more aware of the problem. Much can be done to dispel the notion that the racial playing field in this country is now level. Our sense of Christian morality compels us to do our part in our time in history to ensure that one day, some day, this might in fact become a reality. What we want to say to the Christian Right, however, is that if you want to be taken seriously in your pursuit of moral nation building, then join us in this endeavor.

Poverty

I am personally convinced that, in the long run, history will judge, and should judge, that the years of the War on Poverty constitute one of the noble chapters in American history—noble because the country as a whole, starting with its president, was saying, "We will not tolerate a situation where the many who are okay say it's not their business to be concerned about those who are not." (Hyman Bookbinder, member of the Poverty Task Force that drafted the legislation)[12]

As important as liberal Christians believe the War on Poverty, launched in 1964, was, one of its weaknesses was that it did not effectively put a human face on "poverty." It remained an impersonal concept rather than being understood as people living in unacceptable conditions in a rich nation. Poor people are PEOPLE, and they are who liberal Christians think about when we think about poverty. We see faces like Mrs. Elliott, an 80-year-old woman to whom some of us carried wood in 1976. That winter she had no way to stay warm, except to have a neighbor break up her furniture to use in her tin heater. We see the face of Mr. Baise whose hovel of a home had most of the floor missing when we took wood to him. We see the faces of hundreds of children we saw over a ten-year period when we were making these wood deliveries we knew were only a Band-Aid for a severe problem of being poor in Lynchburg, Virginia. We sent out a call for help to all the city churches. Jerry Falwell's Thomas Road Baptist Church didn't respond. It would seem that he was too busy saving the moral character of the nation to spend any time helping the poor of his hometown.

Poor people are people. That is why liberal Christians get upset when the Christian Right talks about America's moral decline but seems unmoved and unconcerned by reports such as one released in the spring of 2003 by the Children's Defense Fund. It found that the number of black children living in extreme poverty had risen to its highest point since 1979, the earliest data available for comparison. "Extreme poverty" is defined by the CDF as a family of three living with an after tax income of below half the government designation for poverty of $14,128.[13] We can spend the rest of our lives debating poverty, but there is no denying the fact that it is a moral failure for a family of three in this country today with an annual income after taxes of $15,000 to be considered NOT poor, or that it is acceptable that 1.4 million Americans, half of them children, fell into poverty in 2002.[14]

As liberal Christians we believe this is a scandal that should put all of us to shame. More to the point, we believe the War on Poverty launched by our nation in 1964 was indeed a momentous event that should never be forgotten. Out of it came the enormously successful Head Start Program that is now under attack by the radical right led by Tom Delay and company in Congress. In addition, the War on Poverty created Community Action Councils all around the country to help the poorest of the poor and the VISTA (Volunteers In Service To America) program. Nearly all low-income housing that has raised the quality of life for millions of American poor was built during this time. Of course mistakes were made, but the notion that all we have to show for the War on Poverty is more poverty is shameful disregard for the progress that can be made when resources are committed to help poor people.

What strikes us as astounding about the Christian Right is their having to be convinced that helping the poor is what Christians are called to do. A Christian Right professor of journalism at the University of Texas, Marvin Olasky, has written extensively "extolling religious charity as a moral alternative to the sinful welfare state."[15] His is the philosophy behind the "compassionate conservatism" of the Bush administration's approach to helping the nation's poor. The problem is that what we are seeing is a lot of "conservatism" and very little "compassion," as tax cuts that mostly benefit the absurdly wealthy, combined with cuts to every social program, including Bush's own "No Child Left Behind" educational plan and "Faith Based" Initiatives demonstrate. Indeed, the lack of "compassion" was a key factor in the resignation of John Dilulio, the first director of the White House Office of Faith-Based and Community Initiatives. "There is," he wrote in a seven-page letter, "a virtual absence as yet of any policy accomplishments that might, to a fair-minded nonpartisan, count as the flesh on the bones of so-called compassionate conservatism."[16]

Our question is why isn't the Christian Right calling on the administration it so strongly supports to do better. But we think we know the answer. Their "compassionate conservatism" is also more about "conservatism" than "compassion." They say they are concerned about the poor, but do not believe government welfare programs are the answer. Yet they have no hesitancy in supporting corporate welfare that gives billions of dollars in tax breaks with no evidence such breaks give back what they take from communities. Many Christian Right legislators across the nation who are outspoken critics of welfare, are among the strongest supporters for taxpayer-funded stadiums. As liberal Christians we will continue to raise the issue of morality when a professional football team offers its quarterback a contract for $102 million dollars while its billionaire owner insists, at a time when the state has a four-billion-dollar-deficit, that the public should build a new stadium.[17]

We have the ability to show the poor of this country a better way to live and then offer a helping hand to allow them to get there. What we lack is the will. Many of this nation's poor also lack the will because poverty kills the spirit of both those in need and those who can help. This is the factor most ignored and most egregious in its impact on keeping the status quo. Liberal Christians know first hand the difficult job helping the poor can be because we are the ones on the front line doing it. We have seen steps forward taken one day and steps backward the next. But we are committed to keep walking because that is what we believe the Lord of our faith calls us to do. That is reason enough. We are not in the business of assigning people places in the Kingdom of God. Indeed, we recall that Jesus said nothing about the matters the Christian Right sees as paramount, but he did say the dividing line between the people who please God and those who do not is determined by our desire to help the "least of these" (Matthew 25:31ff). We think the Christian Right would be well served to read this text, and then come join us in the work.

AIDS

Acquired Immune Deficiency Syndrome (AIDS) has been around long enough that the panic and fear about it has declined, while the serious threat it poses to the world has not. In 2003 the global HIV/AIDS epidemic killed more than three million people. An estimated five million more acquired the HIV virus, bringing to forty million the number of people living with the virus around the world. AIDS is an epidemic, especially in Africa where thousands of children and adults are infected and dying from it. Some estimates say close to 40 percent of the population of South Africa are infected. Overall, in the worst hit regions of the world AIDS threatens the very fabric of their societies, with life expectancy plummeting. In more developed nations where AIDS is still relatively new, such as Eastern Europe and much of Asia, the HIV virus is rapidly expanding. Here in the U.S. drug users and promiscuous homosexuals and heterosexuals, including teenagers, are among the ones most at risk.

Numerous organizations and foundations are responding to the crisis. The Bill and Melinda Gates Foundation has pledged $200 million over the next five years to fight the disease in India alone. The International Labor Organization has called for employers, governments and workers to join forces in the fight against HIV and AIDS. Several multinational companies operating in developing countries have promised to step up their HIV/AIDS treatment and prevention programs in Africa. The first World AIDS Day 2003 whose theme was "Live and Let Live," was held December 1, 2003, celebrating the progress made in the battle against AIDS and highlighting remaining challenges. The United Nations is using its influence and resources to bring attention to the crisis and to encourage its member nations to support AIDS programs in developing countries. The Bush administration has pledged monies to this end, but well below our ability to help.

We believe this is an appeasement to the Christian Right that continues to believe AIDS is God's punishment of homosexuals. The facts show, of course, that heterosexuals are victims as well as homosexuals, but in our opinion that is not the issue. That people are dying of disease is. Both treatment and prevention programs are essential for bringing this epidemic under control. Moralizing the problem isn't. We do not believe AIDS is a sermon topic for moralizing those who suffer from it. Instead, we see it as an opportunity to join forces with people of all religions and political persuasions to marshal the forces of compassion within the human spirit to save lives. What possible gain the Christian Right sees in its attitude about AIDS escapes us completely. When people are dying, the only thing that matters is helping them, especially when so many of them are children.

Christians can do much to bring focus to what is happening around the world and to contribute resources to the fight against AIDS. We can also bring political pressure on our government to stop politicizing the epidemic and use its considerable financial and political power to confront its spread. It is the morally right thing to do.

Universal Health Care

The lack of health care for 44,000 Americans[18] and the outrageous costs to everyone is not just a health issue. It is a moral problem. "In a morally responsible country," writes Ezekiel J. Emanuel and Victor R. Fuchs, "everyone should have health insurance."[19] Emanuel is an oncologist and bio-ethicist and Fuchs is professor emeritus of economics at Stanford. Combining good medicine and good economics, they are advocates for universal health care vouchers, one among numerous possible solutions to the health care problem in this country waiting for the political will to be implemented. In their own words,

> Each family or individual would be given a voucher to purchase a policy that covered basic services, including doctor visits, hospitalization, pharmacy benefits, some mental health and dental care, and catastrophic coverage. People who want more services, like wider choices of specialists, could pay a premium over the basic voucher. This would continue to be a decentralized system with existing health plans contracting with providers, but their insurance would no longer be employment-based.[20]

The authors believe the current employment-based insurance is a relic of the post-WWII era that had the advantage of grouping workers together for lower costs but the disadvantage of locking them into jobs because of the fear of losing health care benefits. Moreover, costs have not been held down, but passed on to employers and higher and higher worker co-pays.

Emanuel and Fuchs argue that new Medicare enrollees could be part of the voucher system immediately, while existing beneficiaries could remain in the old program until enrollment dropped to a level allowing them to be amalgamated into the voucher plan. But could vouchers prevent insurance companies from avoiding those who need care as a way to hold down costs and increase profits? Emanuel and Fuchs respond by arguing:

> Requiring each insurance company to offer a basic package with catastrophic coverage would insure that individuals with greater needs would not be excluded. More important, the voucher system would pay insurers part of their cost as a lump sum and part as a reimbursement fee for actual services rendered, reducing the incentive for insurers to avoid sick patients. [21]

A national health policy board would administer the system, including certifying health plans and insurance companies, managing the vouchers and payments and collecting and disseminating data on the quality of care.[22]

They further assert:

> The United States now spends about $1.4 trillion on health care. The government already pays about 45 percent of that. In 2003, the average health insurance premium for a family of four is about $9,000. Using that figure and population numbers, a universal health care voucher system would cost about $840 billion, excluding Medicare. That would leave substantial sums for individuals to pay for out-of-pocket expenses and services not in the basic package.
>
> More important, using an earmarked tax to pay for the vouchers would limit cost increases. The level of the tax would determine the value of the voucher. If

the public began demanding an increase in the voucher value, it would be directly linked to higher taxes, moderating these demands and health care inflation.[23]

This description of the voucher health care plan may not be the answer to the crisis we are facing as a nation, but that is not really the point. Rather, our concern is that something must be done about the inequities of health care today, and this idea is one among several showing a solution is possible. The problem is the lack of concern among those of us who have health care, albeit at a high price. Liberal Christians believe 44 million people living without health care in the richest nation in the world is an intolerable injustice. More than that, though, it is an injustice radical political conservatives seem content to do nothing about in the name of the free-market system. Health care is not a privilege in a morally responsible nation, as Emanuel and Fuchs argue. It is a right, and can happen if our society is responsible enough to do something about it. As liberal Christians we experience "cognitive dissonance" whenever we hear the Christian Right leaders campaign against proposals that would end the practice of insurance bean counters making decisions about who gets what care. Nothing in the Bible is more ubiquitous or uncompromising than justice for the marginalized. That so many go to work every day but cannot afford to go to a doctor should not be tolerated by any nation, certainly not one whose majority of citizens claim to believe in God.

Sexism

Discrimination is not limited to race. It happens because of gender and sexual orientation. Instead of telling women to do their "wifely" duties and obey their husbands, the Christian Right should join us in exposing the "glass ceiling" in business and church that tries to keep women in their place. The issue is civil rights. Women pay taxes just as men do. The church should be the loudest voice insisting that unless our nation wants to exempt all women from paying taxes, then it must ensure that all women have equal access to the same jobs and pay as men. Scripture deserves better than to be used to justify discrimination against women in the workplace. Just as the Bible was once used as an argument in favor of slavery, so now it is used by the Christian Right to promote "family values" at the expense of women. Their words ring hollow. Discrimination cannot promote anything of "value," and certainly cannot strengthen the family.

What astounds us is the way the Christian Right promotes patriotism without the slightest hesitation in supporting discrimination against the majority of the population in this country. Women make up over half of this nation, yet have to fight for equal treatment under the law. That there is something wrong with this picture seems obvious to us. It does not matter to us if Christian Right women such as Phyllis Schlafly support discrimination against women; discrimination is wrong. What is more, Shlafley and others most often discriminate from a position of power and wealth. Women living in poverty or barely able to keep their head above water are too busy coping with the effects of discrimination to support it in the name of family preservation.

What is true about sexism regarding women is also true for homosexuals. The Christian Right seems oblivious or unconcerned with civil liberties for homosexual persons. Their view of morality justifies open discrimination, especially when it comes to same-sex marriage. That they do not want to perform same-sex marriages is their right. But to argue for a constitutional amendment that forbids any form of legal union moves the debate from morality to civil rights. Without legal status, gay and lesbian partners have no rights afforded heterosexual unions. A gay man, for example, whose partner was critically ill, was denied access to hospital visitation by the dying man's family who refused to confront their son's homosexuality. This is only one example of numerous ways homosexual partners are not allowed equal treatment under the law.

Liberal Christians are certainly not of one mind about how Christians should respond to this difficult issue. A recent Pew Research survey found that the majority of mainline Protestants oppose same-sex marriages, indicative of where the nation as a whole stands.[24] At the same time, the survey also found that the majority of Americans believe discrimination on the basis of sexual orientation is wrong.

The survey underscores how the debate over societal acceptance of homosexuality has shifted since the mid-'80s. The public has moved decisively in the direction of tolerance on many questions; in particular, discrimination against homosexuals is now widely opposed. This is seen in long-term trends in surveys conducted by the Pew Research Center and by the Gallup Organization. And the current survey shows that a majority of Americans (54%) feel that gay and lesbian couples can be as good a parents as heterosexual couples.[25]

It is obvious that most Americans are perplexed about the right thing to do in regard to rights for homosexuals. Thus, while most liberal Christians support the U.S. Supreme Court's Texas ruling that struck down an archaic sodomy law, the recent Massachusetts Supreme Court ruling allowing same-sex marriages has created a conundrum regarding the national implications of the ruling.[26] As expected, the ruling set off a firestorm of protest by the Christian Right, not least Jerry Falwell. Just after the ruling he stated in his "Falwell Confidential" email that he was redoubling efforts for the constitutional amendment, explaining,

> As the enemies of conventional marriage continue to make gains, it is becoming increasingly imperative that Americans who want to preserve our traditional values must get proactive…Hegemonic jurists will have the leeway to enact their valueless vision on America in terms of altering marriage unless the Federal Marriage Amendment becomes the law of the land.[27]

The distressing part of this kind of reductionist language is that it detracts from the serious and thoughtful debate such matters as this one need. Indeed, as well-known political observer Larry Sabato of the University of Virginia noted in response to the Falwell comments, "This is a lot of sound and fury signifying very little because Virginia is not going to recognize gay marriage and is not going to recognize gay civil unions unless ordered to by the Supreme Court, and if that ever happened, it will be years away."[28]

A more thoughtful response to the Massachusetts ruling came from liberal Christians in Falwell's backyard. A lay leader of a Lynchburg church described the approach his church takes on such issues this way: "I think our history on issues of controversy is that we study them together, looking at all sides of an issue, and then focus on what God calls us to do."[29] Another lay leader from the church commented, "There's never unanimity of opinion about anything like this." A third one agreed, adding that "people stay in the church because of the dialogue. We like a lot of study. It's a real stimulating place to be."[30]

These responses are typical of liberal Christians precisely because we are not dogmatic about homosexuality or other controversial issues. We live with the tension of competing values, making it difficult for us to reconcile religious convictions with civil liberties. In short, we are uncomfortable with religious views serving as the sole basis for denying homosexuals their rights as citizens of this country. We know the history of this kind of legislation. Until recently women lost their legal identity when they married. Only twenty years ago husbands were exempt from rape charges because the prevailing laws did not consent to a wife having the right to say no to forced sex by her husband. At one point states could control the sale of contraceptives or the race of one's chosen partner.[31] It seems that each time these "morally" based laws are struck down Christian Righters say it is another blow to traditional marriage.

But not all conservatives want to characterize same-sex marriage in this way. Columnist David Brooks believes conservatives should encourage gay marriages, not oppose them. In a *New York Times* column, he argues that marriage is in such a crisis today because it relies on a "culture of fidelity," while we live in a "culture of contingency." Men "trade up" for younger trophy wives, and men and women both opt out of marriages when their "needs" are not being met at the moment. Brooks wonders why conservatives don't support gay and lesbian marriage as a way to strengthen the culture of fidelity.

You would think that faced with this marriage crisis, we conservatives would do everything in our power to move as many people as possible from the path of contingency to the path of fidelity. But instead, many argue that gays must be banished from matrimony because gay marriage would weaken all marriage. A marriage is between a man and a woman, they say. It is women who domesticate men and make marriage work.

Well, if women really domesticated men, heterosexual marriage wouldn't be in crisis. In truth, it's moral commitment, renewed every day through faithfulness, that "domesticates" all people...

The conservative course is not to banish gay people from making such commitments. It is to expect that they make such commitments. We shouldn't just allow gay marriage. We should insist on gay marriage. We should regard it as scandalous that two people could claim to love each other and not want to sanctify their love with marriage and fidelity.

When liberals argue for gay marriage, they make it sound like a really good employee benefits plan. Or they frame it as a civil rights issue, like extending the right to vote.

Marriage is not voting. It's going to be up to conservatives to make the important, moral case for marriage, including gay marriage. Not making it means drifting further into the culture of contingency, which, when it comes to intimate and sacred relations, is an abomination.[32]

How ironic that a conservative would indict both the Christian Right and liberal Christians for their position on same-sex marriage. At the least Brooks shows that reasoned discussion advances the debate more than inflammatory rhetoric. As liberal Christians, we are willing to consider the weaknesses of our own position on this issue. If the Christian Right is to do the same, it will have to give up its need to legislate its view of morality, a need and desire made quite clear by Phyllis Schlafly in a column she wrote after the Supreme Court's Texas ruling:

This spring, the Supreme Court dealt devastating blows to longstanding American laws and beliefs about morals and about a just society, and did this without advancing any argument that reasonably relates to the U.S. Constitution. The Court struck down our right to legislate against immoral actions (*Lawrence v. Texas*).[33]

This is the kind of viewpoint that makes understanding impossible. As liberal Christians, we believe legitimate differences of opinion can exist in regard to same-sex marriage—making dialogue, rather than dogma, our choice for the best way to achieve consensus at some level. Until then, we will continue to work for the elimination of sexism in any form.

Violence

Thanks in part to the Christian Right in Minnesota, churches must post a "No Guns Allowed on Premises" sign in a prominent place and also provide a written copy of our policy to anyone packing a pistol. The Christian Right gun-toting legislator who sponsored the "conceal and carry" legislation says she plans to carry her piece everywhere she goes.[34]

We understand why the NRA pushes conceal and carry laws. They've never met a gun they didn't like. We just can't figure out why the Christian Right does. It's not as if we've never been down this road before. It was called "the wild, wild West." When Wyatt Earp banned guns in Tucson, he apparently knew something the NRA and the Christian Right don't, or don't want to. More guns in more hands doesn't make for less crime. No reliable data exists that shows gun-toting states have seen a drop in violent crimes. The only reason people want to carry a gun is…they want to! That's it. Drunks at football games want to. Parents who want to kill Little League umpires want to. Drivers prone to road rage want to. Women who think pulling a gun on a robber doesn't increase the odds THEY will be killed want to. All these people support conceal and carry laws, not because they are needed or advisable. They just want to.

This issue underscores how shortsighted the Christian Right is. They support more guns on the street but say precious little about the violence they cause. About all they do say is what the NRA says, "Guns don't kill people; people kill people." They want to believe that we live in a civilized society that sets the standard for living the rest of the world needs to emulate. Why would other nations want to follow the U.S. in being the most violent developed nation on Earth? What example is it to be number one in murders and violent crimes while states are passing laws to put guns in the hands of more people? Using the logic that guns don't kill people but people do, Americans must be a troubled bunch, and hate more than most. We lead the industrialized world in gun-related deaths. We're also number one in children under fifteen dying from non-war gunfire, number one in the suicide rate of kids under fifteen, number one in executing children convicted of violent crimes, number one in recorded rapes. In fact, we are number one in numerous categories no country wants to be number one in.[35]

It is an enigma why Americans think this nation models a quality of life that is the envy of the world. The only people who want to live here are those who live in despotic and desperate circumstances. Citizens from developed countries see it as a nice place to visit, but they definitely don't want to live here. The reality is that this nation is majority Christian, yet is the most violent developed nation on Earth. Not much of a Christian witness in that. Yet the Christian Right seems to believe the only violence that counts is abortion. They are against gun control and for capital punishment, but they believe abortion is murder, without regard to circumstances. They believe in putting teenagers to death by lethal injection, but they want doctors who perform abortions to be put into prison.

Violence is a major issue in America today, but the Christian Right is too busy trying to post the Ten Commandments in courthouses to notice. Kids are killing kids on school grounds, but the Christian Right is too busy making sure they pray every morning in the classroom before the violence begins. Is this being too critical? We don't think so. Parody underscores the absurdity of their positions. They are worried about saving people's souls, but don't seem at all disturbed by the social inequities that nurture violence that kills the body. The problem with the Christian Right is that they don't see the forest for the trees. They think the moral fiber of the nation is going down the tubes, but you don't need 20/20 vision to see that. Social ills do not account fully for moral failure, but to pretend that they play no role is to be intentionally blind. The correlation between poverty and violence, poverty and illegitimate births, poverty and abandoned children, poverty and drug abuse is well documented. It simply is not true that individual character alone determines one's future. Being a liberal Christian means taking seriously the social roots of personal behavior and achievement. We wonder why this is so difficult for the Christian Right.

Militarism

During the 2003 tensions with North Korea over its restarting of a nuclear arms development program, former White House Press Secretary Ari Fleshner criticized the North Korean government for wasting money on arming itself with nuclear weapons while letting its own people suffer economically. It was good advice, another example of how our government, with the strong flag-waving support of the Christian Right, sees the speck in someone else's eye while missing the plank in its own. The Bush administration's proposed 2004 fiscal year budget for U.S. military spending is $379 billion, an increase of $48 billion over 2003. As one person characterized this increase, "Adding $48 billion to the Pentagon budget is like providing an overweight person with dozens of fat-filled desserts."[36] Moreover, the 2004 proposed budget is more than the combined spending of all U.S. allies combined.

In contrast to the Pentagon getting enough money to buy anything and everything each branch of the military really wants, state and the federal governments are cutting social programs across the board in the name of budgetary restraints. Yet the combined spending of these programs does not match military spending for 2003, and if proposals are enacted, they will continue to decrease while the Pentagon gets more and more. It's a fairly simple thing to understand. At a time when taxes have been cut and military spending is increasing at an unprecedented rate, the money has to come from somewhere.

In fact, it does. Military spending increases at the expense of social programs.

The rationale is that we must increase military spending for the sake of the war on terrorism. That would be a good argument if it had any truth to it, but the reality is, we are buying weapons we don't need and will not help in this kind of war. A case in point is missile defense. Just when many liberal Christians thought "Star Wars" was dead, the current administration is proceeding to build such a system, albeit in a more limited scope, without any reliable evidence it will work. Indeed, there is much more credible evidence it does not and cannot simply because there are too many variables that will always make the system vulnerable. For missile defense to be worth the cost and risks, it must be full-proof. But that is not even the real reason this high-tech adventure that will cost more than a trillion dollars before it is deployed is such a waste. The thing is not needed. Terrorists are not going to launch an intercontinental ballistic missile to attack us. They are going to fly planes in buildings, or leave a suitcase bomb on the sidewalk or in a subway. Further, no rogue nation would do such a thing because they know we will know where it came from and will blow them off the face of the Earth.

This is not rocket science. Common sense is sufficient to see the folly of our mixed up social priorities. But don't take our word for it. Listen to the words of President Eisenhower, who knew a thing or two about war and peace from his address, "The Chance for Peace," delivered before the American Society of Newspaper Editors on April 16, 1953:

> Every gun that is made, every warship launched, every rocket fired signifies, in the final sense, a theft from those who hunger and are not fed, those who are cold and are not clothed. This world in arms is not spending money alone. It is spending the sweat of its laborers, the genius of its scientists, the hopes of its children.
>
> The cost of one modern heavy bomber is this: a modern brick school in more than 30 cities.
>
> It is two electric power plants, each serving a town of 60,000 population.

It is two fine, fully equipped hospitals.
It is some 50 miles of concrete highway.
We pay for a single fighter with a half million bushels of wheat.
We pay for a single destroyer with new homes that could have housed more than 8,000 people.
This, I repeat, is the best way of life to be found on the road the world has been taking.
This is not a way of life at all, in any true sense. Under the cloud of threatening war, it is humanity hanging from a cross of iron.

Eight years later he would say good-bye to the nation in January, 1961, in a speech remembered for its warning against the undue influence of a "military industrial complex" the cold war had made necessary, but which itself was also a threat to our way of life:

This conjunction of an immense military establishment and a large arms industry is new in the American experience. The total influence—economic, political, even spiritual—is felt in every city, every state house, every office of the Federal government. We recognize the imperative need for this development. Yet we must not fail to comprehend its grave implications. Our toil, resources and livelihood are all involved; so is the very structure of our society.

The challenge this new world presented, Eisenhower believed, was how to balance military needs with liberties and democratic process. He clearly believed that a society dominated by a military-industrial complex posed a serious threat to both. His concluding statements in his farewell to the nation bears remembering: "We cannot mortgage the material assets of our grandchildren without risking the loss of their political and spiritual heritage. We want democracy to survive for all generations to come, not to become the insolvent phantom of tomorrow."

As liberal Christians we believe Eisenhower's warning continues to be relevant today. If anything, the military-industrial complex threat he warned against is more ominous than ever. "A nation's hope of lasting peace," he also said in that speech, "cannot be firmly based upon any race in armaments but rather upon just relations and honest understanding with all other nations." We believe our government has all but abandoned this counsel. How the Christian Right can support this turn of events escapes us. That it does makes us more determined to expose the extremist views they represent. We believe a strong military is a practical means of stabilizing relations between enemy nations, but we believe with equal fervor that militarism is also a threat to peace. In a nation as wealthy as ours, as liberal Christians we believe that an ideology that promotes taking from the least to build weapons we do not need is an intolerable obscenity.

The Environment

It is now being predicted that by 2050 the world's population will increase by one billion. Natural resources are already being strained, and yet the industrialized nations play games with treaties that could serve as a step toward becoming responsible stewards of the Earth. The United States is the leading game player, but the current administration has withdrawn from the Kyoto protocol. This treaty, negotiated by more than 100 countries over a decade, calls for the 38 largest industrial nations to reduce their emissions of greenhouse gases by 2012 to 5.2 percent below the levels in 1990. The stated reason for the U. S. withdrawal was that it didn't go far enough and would negatively impact U.S. economic growth. The administration said it could do better, and would. Thus far it has done nothing. Not something. Nothing! No revisions have been suggested, no new conference to forge a new agreement has been called. What is emerging is what liberal Christians suspected all along. The treaty was opposed by the powerful energy lobby.

We do not believe the Kyoto Treaty would save the environment. It clearly will not. But it would have been a means to a greater end, a first step opening the door to serious international laws to protect the world's resources from exploitation and irreparable damage. With the U.S. opting out, however, the door has been effectively shut. A world agreement on environmental protection without the signature of the world's number one polluter is an impotent treaty. That is what we have done to Kyoto.

The shortsightedness of our government's actions boggles the mind. A recent *New York Times* editorial sought to underscore the ecological disaster the world is now facing. Even though no scholarly study has disputed the gradual rise in global temperatures over the past century, the editorial noted that it seems to take an occasional news flash from some remote corner of the globe documenting startling changes in landscapes to get people's attention. It cited the report two years ago "that the snows of Kilimanjaro, which inspired Ernest Hemingway's famous short story, could vanish in fifteen years, and that the seemingly indestructible glaciers in the Bolivian Andes might not last another ten." Further, last year "brought evidence of disturbing and apparently irreversible changes in Alaska's environment—melting permafrost, sagging roads, dying forests—arising from an astonishing rise of 5.4 degrees in Alaska's average temperature over the past thirty years."

But the worst, the *Times* said, was yet to come. It then summarized the latest bad news.

A report from three scientists that the Arctic's largest ice shelf—a 150-square-mile, 100-foot-thick mass of ice that has been sitting more or less intact off the northern Canadian coast for 3,000 years—is disintegrating. The scientists say the breakup results from a century-long warming trend that has accelerated in the last two years. It is not yet possible, they say, to tie the melting directly to rising atmospheric concentrations of so-called greenhouse gases, or to the human activities— chiefly the burning of fossil fuels like coal and oil—that create these gases. But they warn that a "critical threshold" has been breached, and that on the other side of this threshold lie abrupt changes in natural conditions we have long taken for granted.[37]

In light of these realities, it takes burying one's head in the sand to believe global warming is a liberal creation. Rather, it is a fact supported by mounting scientific data that is an indictment of people who will believe it only when it is too late for all of us. Even the Bush administration that has relaxed enforcement of all major environmental regulations passed under both Republican and Democratic administrations has admitted that global warming might be a reality, but their answer is to adjust to it and get over it. No change in attitudes or policies. Just live with it.

Except this is precisely what we cannot do—live with it. The Earth isn't always a friendly place, and when human beings monkey around with it, we invariably get the short end of the stick. As Christians we are unwilling to watch this rape take place without trying to stop it. Production and consumption combined with pollution are out of control and we believe there is much that can be done to bring this chaos under control. Unlike the Christian Right, we are not fatalists. We do not believe everything taking place is part of some grand scheme of God's preparing the world for its end. On the contrary, we believe people are living as if we are the creators of the Earth rather than its stewards. We are destroying land and water and air as if we laid the foundations of the Earth and can do anything we choose to do. We are guilty of idolatry. The consequences of adding a billion more of us to the mix are unthinkable.

If any group should be sounding the alarm about what is happening, it should be the Christian community. We are the ones who believe the Earth came into existence by intention rather than accident, that it has design and purpose and beauty not of our own making. We are the ones who believe human beings have been charged with the responsibility of stewardship. That the Christian Right supports relaxation of environmental laws and standards in the name of economic expansion or military needs contradicts the biblical imperative to treat the Earth with respect and wisdom. The primary cause of pollution is greed and selfishness. If it didn't cost anything corporately or personally to clean it up and keep it clean, it would be done. Environmental protection is not a liberal cause. It is a Christian obligation.

This is why liberal Christians are committed to efforts that can protect the Earth's limited resources, such as those initiated by "The Earth Charter—USA." Its purpose is to grow respect of life and the environment by inviting individuals and groups to join them in adopting and promoting the values of "The Earth Charter" they have written. It is a marvelous statement of responsible citizenship that every Christian ought to be anxious to affirm. The Charter is divided into four categories: Respect and Care for the Community of Life; Ecological Integrity; Social and Economic Justice; and Democracy, Nonviolence, and Peace. Category one calls for compassion, an awareness of the interdependence of all life, and a willingness to work to establish democratic communities that are just and peaceful. Category two calls on communities, states, and nations to make environmental conservation and rehabilitation integral to developmental plans, and to educate the public on consumption and waste issues. Category three connects protection of the Earth with matters of social and economic justice and issues of human rights. The final category supports the strengthening of democratic institutions at all levels in which tolerance, nonviolence, and peace are valued and promoted.[38]

Beyond "The Earth Charter" itself, the rationale for it also seems to us to be a statement for every Christian. In part it says,

> Life often involves tensions between important values. This can mean difficult choices. However, we must find ways to harmonize diversity with unity, the exercise of freedom with the common good, short-term objectives with long-term goals. Every individual, family, organization, and community has a vital role to play. The arts, sciences, religions, educational institutions, media, businesses, non-governmental organizations, and governments are all called to offer effective leadership. The partnership of government, civil society, and business is essential for effective governance.[39]

If the Christian Right is truly concerned about the future of life here on Earth, it should be willing to speak in favor of this kind of thinking and the kind of work Earth Charter–USA is doing. But don't bet money on it. The rationale for the "Charter" also calls on all nations to renew their commitment to the United Nations and fulfill their obligations under existing international agreements and also support implementation of the Charter's principles in such a way that they become an international legally binding instrument for future development.[40] The Christian Right sees the United Nations as a code word for "liberal conspiracy" and, thus, will have nothing to do with The Earth Charter or other programs thought up by liberals.

We take a measure of pride in standing at the opposite end of the spectrum. Whether one supports Earth Charter–USA in particular is not the point. That Christians join with all peoples in efforts to promote environmental stewardship is. This is one of the most pressing issues of our time. Nature is not forgiving. Damage it and a price is paid. Do irreparable harm to the Earth and we all die. It really is that simple. To support short-term gain government policies at the expense of long-term care of the environment is collective suicide. If believing this makes us liberal Christians, then that is who and what we are. And proud of it!

13

THE LIBERAL CHRISTIAN'S MANIFESTO

It may seem a bit bold, if not off putting, to call what we believe a "manifesto," but we do so only in the literal sense of the word which means "a public declaration." We believe it is time—indeed, past time—for liberal Christians to stop being ashamed of who we are, stop being afraid of the current conservative climate, stop being on the defensive for the things we believe. It is, instead, a time to speak of what we believe that offers an alternative Christian view to what is usually in the headlines. It is an alternative grounded in the hope that Christianity can be a force for peace and justice around the world. While there is much to criticize about the Christian Right, as we have shown, it is equally important to speak positively about the alternative.

The Liberal Christian Manifesto

We declare before God and all humanity that as liberal Christians we are witnesses to the gospel of Jesus Christ.

We, therefore, believe that being God's people doesn't mean we are the only people of God.

We believe the Bible is a moral guide rather than a book of rules.

We believe in life *before* death as well as after.

We believe the many forms of diversity among people
are to be celebrated rather than feared.
We believe God blesses other nations as well as
America.
We believe working on behalf of peace, justice, and
compassion is the way of Jesus.
We believe in telling all the truth we know without
claiming to know all the truth there is.

The value of succinctness does not allow for a thorough
explanation of the theological concerns to which these
statements point. Nor is such detail all that important to our
case against the Christian Right. At the same time the Manifesto
does deserve some explanation.

*We declare before God and all humanity that as liberal
Christians we are witnesses to the gospel of Jesus Christ.*

This is a clear affirmation of our commitment to viewing
the world through Christian lenses while intentionally
witnessing to the One to whom we are committed. In short,
this statement says that we are thoroughly Christian. We have
come to know God through Jesus Christ. We have no hesitancy
in speaking of that which we believe to be true. This is
important because of two extremes between which we find
ourselves. On one end is the Christian Right that judges our
Christianity as inadequate. It sees us as betrayers of authentic
Christianity and not worthy of the name "Christian." This first
line of the Manifesto challenges their judgmentalism. Being
liberal does not make us reluctant to tell who we are. We believe
that being Christian is what we bring to the table of interfaith
dialogue, and we have no desire to be coy or embarrassed
about it. On the contrary, the answer to the Christian Right is
to make a more winsome Christian witness, not to hide this
fact. So we declare first as liberal Christians that we are
"Christian" and have a passion about this identity.

Indirectly it also suggests that we are tired of the Christian
Right appointing themselves as judge of who is and is not a
genuine Christian. Some of the negative responses to our
Falwell article ironically criticized us for going public with
our criticism of the Christian Right. They thought this gave

the "enemies" of Christianity more "ammunition," an interesting choice of words. Our reply is that the Christian Right seems not the least hesitant to state their judgments about us. More important, though, it is precisely in the public arena that the Christian Right needs to be criticized. They are Christian extremists who we hope do not represent the majority of Christians in this country. They simply have the loudest voices and are quite willing to engage in ugly debate on television and radio programs that encourage incivility.

We, therefore, believe that being God's people doesn't mean we are the only people of God.

One week before Ramadan, the Muslim holy month of fasting, worship and contemplation, a writer who reports on churches wrote the following regarding her visit to a fundamentalist church.

> The husband-wife ministry team at Life Church lamented that Muslims had not accepted Jesus Christ. "The world doesn't need more religion, said the Rev. Dale Sisam. Next week the Muslims are going to be fasting and praying, but they don't know for what. I pray they'll find Jesus.
>
> Moments later the Rev. Sandy Sisam threw out a challenge: "If they're going to pray and fast next week, let us pray and fast this week that the Muslims will find Jesus Christ. Fasting need not entail giving up food, she said: "I fasted Starbucks last week, and I love my lattes!"
>
> The message is clear: Accept Jesus or face damnation. "Those who reject Christ will receive everlasting punishment and eternal separation from the presence of God," one handout reads.[1]

This is the attitude liberal Christians not only do not share, but find lacking in biblical foundation unless one chooses, as we have noted, to take two verses out of context to overshadow everything else Jesus said. But the absolutism it represents is the bread and butter of the Christian Right.

Our rejection of this kind of thinking is greeted, of course, with the charge that we are not really Christians in what we believe. In fact, it is precisely because our Manifesto begins with an affirmation of our faith in Jesus as Savior and Lord that we believe being people of God does not mean we have to be the only people of God. Further, we intend for this statement to be a direct challenge to the Christian Right. Its members believe that being God's people not only requires one to be a Christian, but the kind of Christian they are, believing the things they believe. We do not agree. We take the position that God is bigger than any human understanding of God. Belonging to God is a choice we have made, but it is not one available only to us as liberal Christians. We think the Christian Right has made God into a Christian, committing what we consider to be a primary theological error, namely, seeking to limit the sovereignty of God on the basis of their very fallible interpretation of scripture (see chapter 4). We reject their claim as the only people of God and the way they read two passages of scripture to justify it. The first is purportedly the words of Jesus who said that he was the way, the truth, and the life, and that no one comes to God except through the son (14:6). The other is from the disciple Peter who said that no other name than that of Jesus had the power to save (Acts 4:12).

These two verses have been interpreted in numerous ways that negate the Christian Right's claim that if you're not a Christian, come Judgment Day you're dead in the water (or the fire, as the case may be). Moreover, some scholars who are also committed Christians have made strong cases that neither Jesus nor Peter actually made either of these statements, which are instead the church's words reflecting the tensions between Jewish Christians and Jews. But for our purposes, applying a little common sense is all that is needed. To begin with, Jesus and Peter were both speaking to Jews because there were no Christians. Christianity didn't exist. The question Jews faced about Jesus was whether or not he was the real Messiah. Others had made the same claim before and after him. So it is quite possible to understand his words as saying, "I am the one." This would also have been Peter's point. No one else who claims to be the Messiah is, only Jesus.

Another question is why Jesus mentioned his being the only way one time, if the eternal fate of all Jews and everyone else depended on it. You would think he would have said something about it a few more times. He talked about being compassionate and loving toward others numerous times. It seems a bit shortsighted to mentioned the linchpin for the world's hope only once. Common sense would suggest that the reason he didn't is because it didn't get to the core of his message. That he was God's "Anointed" was the message, and being God's son meant he was *extending* the blessings of God given to Israel to non-Jews as well.

This suggests that the way the Christian Right interprets these passages contradicts their intended meaning. Rather than trying to establish that Jesus was the only way, it is more likely that they intended to say that Judaism wasn't. As such they were reminders of a basic teaching of Judaism rooted in both God's eternal covenant with Noah that included all people and the promise to Abraham that through his seed all the nations of the Earth would be blessed. This was not a message the Jews of Jesus' day were ready to hear, oppressed as they were by the Romans. Jesus had gotten into trouble in his home town of Nazareth for saying the same thing (Luke 4:16–30). The issue was Jesus' authority, and that depended on the authenticity of his being the Messiah Jews had been expecting.

Unfortunately the Christian Right has turned Jesus' being the Messiah into a Christian dogma that bears little resemblance to who Jesus was. His message was that God was bigger than Judaism and that in God's realm there was neither Jew nor Gentile. This is what liberal Christians believe. We follow a Jesus who was concerned about people knowing how much God loves them, rather than fearing how quickly God will judge them. Knowing the sinfulness of Christians first hand, the claim of our being the only people of God seems unsustainable. Contrary to the Christian Right's assessment of liberalism, we take "sin" very seriously. The fact that we do is why we have no tolerance for their intolerance. Only those sure of their place in God's realm are ready to exclude others.

Sin is self-absorption that leads one to playing God rather than honoring God. We count it a grace to be among the people of God, in our view a gift in no way diminished by its being shared with others whose beliefs are different from our own.

Further, we consider the notion that the validity of Christianity is dependent upon all other religious traditions being false is itself false. In their insistence that Christianity is the only true faith, the Christian Right shares religious exclusivism with Islam that it most fears. Both reject Judaism, their mother faith, each in its own way laying claim to being the only people of God. All the while, Judaism has thrived longer than either without exclusivistic claims. According to the Torah, God's covenant with Noah was universal in its scope. It's a message the children of Judaism would do well to learn. Being people of God only doesn't mean we have to be the only people of God.

> *We believe the Bible is a moral guide rather than a*
> *book of inflexible rules.*

Why we believe the Christian Right is wrong has its origins in the way it reads the Bible, not unlike the fact that the trouble with Islamic fundamentalists lies in the way they read the Qu'ran. We have already discussed differences between the Christian Right and liberal Christians in how each of us reads the Bible. What we can add here is that we refuse to turn it into a rulebook of rigid commands the Christian Right says everyone should follow but don't live up to themselves. That is how they use the Bible to judge the rest of us. Despite claims to the contrary, morality is always contextual. Under normal circumstances, telling the truth is the morally right thing to do. Faced with Hitler's "final solution to the Jewish problem," hiding Jews in your home and lying about it was the morally right thing to do. Stealing someone's car is morally wrong. Stealing a loaf of bread in Rwanda to feed your starving children is not. War is a horrible evil. War may also be justified as a means to stopping a holocaust.

Instead of making the Bible accessible to people, the Christian Right's insistence that it is a rigid moral code— primarily about sex and absolutely in the way they understand it—makes it less than appealing to anyone who understands the ambiguities of life. They rail against "situation ethics" but have little idea of what Joseph Fletcher, its primary author, said about it.[2] "Do whatever you please" not only does not represent the heart of situation ethics, it is a distortion of it. Fletcher was committed to moral codes and standards, saying that one sets aside any moral command in a situation *only* if the cause of love is better served by doing so. Granted, he may have not defined love in the way the Christian Right might want, but the principle seems to us to have more than a little biblical foundation. In both the Hebrew and Christian scriptures love is the goal of a godly life. That is why the apostle Paul said: "The commandments, 'You shall not commit adultery; You shall not murder; You shall not steal; You shall not covet,' and any other commandment, are summed up in this word, 'Love your neighbor as yourself.' Love does no wrong to a neighbor; therefore, love is the fulfilling of the law."

For situation ethics to suggest that it is the morally right thing to do to set aside traditional moral laws when love is better served by doing so seems to us to be something other than a liberal attempt to undermine the Bible. Instead, it is a reasonable means of balancing both commandment and circumstances. To us it is an effort to bring common sense to bear upon the realities of life in a way that honors biblical morality without turning it into a sword on the neck of those who want to live by it. It is too easy to preach the Bible as if it contains a set of moral rules demanding strict obedience. It is something altogether different and more true to life to have to make hard decisions about right and wrong in ambiguous situations. In principle, for example, one may believe abortion is morally wrong, but to suggest the circumstances surrounding a twenty-year-old college co-ed being pregnant as a result of rape makes no difference is itself moral callousness. The Christian Right is like political parties in numerous ways. It seems more interested in sound bites that garner money and votes than offering genuine help to people confronted by the moral complexities of real life. Using the Bible as a rod with which to threaten people will only lead to dismissal rather than serious engagement.

The Bible is full of stories and teachings that provide help with living a life that pleases God. Biblical material that offers moral guidance is welcome aid as we face decisions that will not lend themselves to simplistic sermonizing. If love is the aim to which Christians are to strive (1 Corinthians 14:1), then it only makes sense to draw upon every resource available as we try to apply that principle in all circumstances. Moral principles found in the Bible are important guides to this end. When they become inviolable rules of conduct, however, they become stumbling blocks rather than help. We believe our view that biblical teachings are a moral guide rather than rules to follow is the means by which to ensure that they will have enduring relevance in the changing circumstances of daily life.

We believe in life before death as well as after.

To say that we believe in life *before* death as well as after is intended to highlight the Christian Right's mistaken notion that the motivation for living well today is to avoid eternal punishment in the future. They are more interested in people's souls than in their bodies. Thus, they are quick to offer advice for those who are poor in spirit, but slow to come to the aid of those who are poor. They are anxious to receive anyone who claims to hunger and thirst after righteousness, but they oppose governmental programs that seek to help people who simply hunger and thirst. The Second Coming of Jesus is more important to them than his first appearance. They are confident they will be caught up in a "rapture" (see chapter 4) they believe will transport them to heavenly realms, as if this world has no meaning except to get them ready for the next one.

We, on the other hand, like the world we live in. Scripture, after all, says that at the moment of creation God looked upon all that was made and declared it to be good (Genesis 1:24). From our perspective, life is not something to be endured. It is to be enjoyed. We are to bear fruit and make the most of the days we have. What disturbs us about the Christian Right is their apparent disdain for this world while not hesitating to accumulate the riches it offers. The various empires of Christian Right leaders live on the fat of this land they believe is going to hell in a hand basket. They are the rich of this world in comparison to the abject poverty that exists in other nations, yet they would have us believe their only concern is the Kingdom of God. Not that liberal Christians have not been seduced by the materialism of American capitalism. What distinguishes our sin from theirs is that we do not pretend that material needs don't matter. We consider the quality of life a person experiences *before* death to be part of the gospel's concern for the whole of life. If the Christian Right enjoys eating the fatted calf at gatherings in which they recognize politicians who give tax cuts for the wealthiest Americans, that is their business. But we are determined to do all we can to ensure that the poorest among us get a few slices for their tables.

Our theology is that God's riches are not awaiting us. They are available now. As short as life may be, it is to be lived fully without shame or disdain. The first coming of Jesus included wedding parties and sitting at the table with those living on the fringes of life. We have no way of knowing for sure, but it is our opinion that the Christian Right would not like Jesus very much if they had lived when he did. No one accused of being a glutton and drunkard and associating with sinners would have been a Christian Right favorite (Luke 7:34). Instead, they have made Jesus so holy he loses his earthly appeal to those of us who think being of this world can be a good thing as long as it doesn't go to your head. Focusing on a world to come has no redeeming value for this world we are told God loved enough to send Jesus into (John 3:16).

We believe the many forms of diversity among people are to be celebrated rather than feared.

Our saying that we believe the many forms of diversity among people are to be celebrated rather than feared is one of the reasons the Christian Right describes our views as "godless liberalism." As far as we are concerned their criticism reveals the fact that, to use an old phrase, their God is too small. We believe the rainbow is a metaphor for the human family. All of it, not just the people of whom the Christian Right approves. We celebrate diversity because God is its source. The human family is diverse because God is. The God of our faith is too big to fully comprehend, whereas the God of the Christian Right is small enough to be possessed by people who think they have a corner on truth and goodness. We understand the impulse to make God small. Religious people in every generation have felt this urge. But we see creation in all its diversity as a reminder that God is knowable, yet never fully known. The reason diversity threatens the Christian Right is because they believe in a God who is sovereign on their terms.

Essentially the God of the Christian Right thinks and acts the way they do. It is a common tendency among religious people, as Henry McNeal Turner, a black clergyman of the nineteenth century, argued in an 1898 essay entitled "God is a Negro." He said that because every other race "envisioned God in its image," the "Negro" should "believe that he resembles God as much so as other people."[3] The Christian Right is as guilty of this as the rest of us. Their understanding of God is shaped by who they are even as ours is. But they refuse to admit to this human trait, preferring to insist that diversity has its limits and are quick to identify what they are. This is one of the reasons they are dangerous. America is a culture of diversity. Throughout our history we have rejected efforts to do what the Christian Right wants to do—make this nation into its own image the way they have done with God.

We, on the other hand, do not fear diversity, though at times we may be uncomfortable with its needs and demands. Contrary to what the Christian Right thinks, for example, there is a diversity of views among liberal Christians on issues such as abortion and homosexuality. We are not of one mind about many things, except that we have all had experiences wherein a particular diversity of which we were afraid turned out to be a source of personal enrichment. We believe such moments are the work of the Holy Spirit. We celebrate them in the trust that God is bigger than we can imagine and reveals this fact in unanticipated ways, not least through relationships with people different from us.

Herein is the way fears are overcome. Issues scare people until they meet them in people. This is why the fear of terrorism that now grips Americans will not be overcome by security strategies or compromising basic rights. It will be conquered as we live more deeply into the diverse culture we have become. Diversity is what made this country a sanctuary for people around the world seeking freedom from oppression in its many ugly forms. The fear of diversity is an expression of the desire for everyone to be like us. To label it as loose tolerance is to distort the truth about creation itself. Rainbows are what they are because of their diversity. That is the nature of life. We welcome diversity because it reminds us of the greatness of God. Only those whose God is smaller than they are fear it. We delight in being a part of creation's diversity. We want nothing less for others. That is why we believe it is to be celebrated.

We believe God blesses other nations as well as America.

As the war in Iraq began, a sign in a yard read, "God bless the world." It expressed the kind of sentiment consistent with the way liberal Christians think. If there is only One true God, then by definition the whole world is in God's hands. The United States is included, but God's hands hold more than this country. One might suppose the Christian Right also believes this, but their rhetoric does a good job of hiding it. They see America as "the new Israel," a Christian nation chosen and blessed by God to prepare the way for the Second Coming of Jesus and the end of the world. They stand for freedom and justice for all, so long as you're white, male, straight, and rich. Otherwise you are going to have to fight for your freedom and justice.

Liberal Christians reject the argument that God blesses America especially, or more than other nations. Americans are no better people than anyone else. We have no special role in God's work, nor are we exempt from all the injustices that inflict other nations. Other nations can serve the causes of justice, peace, and freedom just as we can. At times we lead other nations, but we have not learned to follow very well. Our faith says that God has no nationality, nor any favorites. Life is so created that rain and sun and everything in-between comes to the good and bad, the just and unjust, alike (Matthew 5:45). We are quite willing to trust that the goodness of God encompasses all peoples.

We believe one of the reasons the Christian Right contributes to tensions in the world and is providing uncritical support to America's current war on terrorism is that they think this nation shares a covenant with God that ancient Israel shared. They see us as the chosen nation in the modern world with our role to impose on the world a Christian way of life. Any blessing God gives the world will come through us. Thus, when God blesses America, God blesses the world. It is as if the Christian Right wants to be the favored child in the family and cannot trust their parents love if they show love to their sisters and brothers.

As we have already discussed in chapter 8, patriotism and Christian commitment will always be in a relationship of tension for liberal Christians. From our perspective it should be enough for Christians to be grateful that God blesses all peoples. To want something special for ourselves is prideful. So the signs in our yards will always read, "God bless the world."

> *We believe working on behalf of peace, justice,*
> *and compassion is the way of Jesus.*

The Christian Right considers "belief" the essence of what it means to be Christian. We don't. While belief is important, ours is a faith that says actions speak louder than words. We didn't come up with this idea, Jesus did.

> Not everyone who says to me, 'Lord, Lord,' will enter
> the kingdom of heaven, but only the one who does the
> will of my Father in heaven. (Matthew 7:21)

Some of the earliest Christians got the same impression from him we have.

> But be doers of the word, and not merely hearers who
> deceive themselves. For if any are hearers of the word
> and not doers, they are like those who look at
> themselves in a mirror; for they look at themselves and,
> on going away, immediately forget what they were like.
> But those who look into the perfect law, the law of
> liberty, and persevere, being not hearers who forget
> but doers who act—they will be blessed in their doing.
> (James 1:22–25)

Knowing what to do in all situations is not as simple as the Christian Right would have you believe, but we can know enough to keep us busy. Jesus said that the clearest sign of being a Christian is loving others.

I give you a new commandment, that you love one another. Just as I have loved you, you also should love one another. By this everyone will know that you are my disciples, if you have love for one another. (John 13:34–35)

We think translating love into everyday life means working on behalf of peace, justice, and compassion. Other things as well, but at least these. They are the marks of our witness as Christians. Not that peacemaking is easy or simple. Quite the opposite. It is incredibly difficult. But at least it reaches beyond winning battles and wars. Winning peace requires working for justice and showing unconditional compassion. There is no peace without these. That is why it is much harder to win a war than to establish a lasting peace.

Liberal Christians understand the realities of hate and militarism. While some among us are pacifists, others are not. What we share is the commitment to work for peace by doing more than giving lip service to justice and compassion. We are not of one mind as to the position Jesus would take regarding tensions in international relations today and genuine threats to freedom. But we are convinced freedom without justice and compassion is a hollow victory, and that meaningful faith attends to all three.

The current quagmire unfolding in post-war Iraq is a disturbing sign of the truth of which we speak. The easy defeat of an unarmed Iraqi military was not accompanied by a plan to lay the groundwork for justice and compassion in a culture we do not understand. A year after mission was declared accomplished, violence continues to rule the country. Compassion has taken a back seat to security. Justice is all but out of the room entirely. It is both naive and foolish to believe soldiers from a self-proclaimed Christian nation can impose justice on an Islamic culture. Justice must be contextual to work. Codes of conduct and cultural mores cannot be ignored. Yet our government has done little to learn about Islam and Muslim ways. Now we are angry for not being welcomed with open arms as the liberators we envisioned ourselves to be.

We wish the Christian Right would join us in working for peace by taking justice and compassion more seriously. But we confess that we are not holding our breath. They seem content to trust peace to having the biggest sword. We are not. Being Christian is a call to work on behalf of peace, justice, and compassion with equal commitment and energy.

We believe in telling all the truth we know without claiming to know all the truth there is.

It astounds us the way the Christian Right speaks with authority as if it has captured the truth of God without equivocation or complication. They are not content to tell what they know, but insist that what they know is what everyone else must know. As such, their boldness is not to be admired but condemned. It is not courage they demonstrate, but arrogance.

To speak forthrightly about things we believe does not force us into the position of claiming to know truth absolutely. We regularly remind ourselves of the witness who was sworn in with the traditional question, "Do you swear to tell the truth, the whole truth, and nothing but the truth, so help you God?" to which the witness replied, "Sir, if I could tell the truth, the whole truth, and nothing but the truth, I would be God."

Short of claiming to tell the whole truth and nothing but the truth, we are satisfied to tell the truth we know as Christians. None among us possesses an infallible mind that could comprehend infallible truth. Our faith is the respectful of others kind, the "always be ready to make your defense to anyone who demands from you an accounting for the hope that is in you; yet do it with gentleness and reverence" kind (1 Peter 3:15–16). Unafraid to disagree with the beliefs of others religious traditions, we consider disagreement with "gentleness and reverence" to be a good way to relate to one another. Faith does not require Christians to speak as if we know all the truth there is. It is always and at all times seeing through a mirror dimly (1 Corinthians 13:12). It is the human condition. It is also what makes faith necessary. To know truth absolutely replaces the need for faith. By its nature faith is an affirmation always subject to challenge, refinement, and maturation. Christians should have no hesitancy in telling all the truth we know, and no need to know all the truth there is.

So this is our Manifesto, our public statement of faith, our coming out rather than hiding who we are. Within our ranks you will find regular debate about the tenets we have discussed. An open mind never stops asking questions or challenging established points of view. The consensus among liberal Christians will never be achieved on the basis of doctrinal agreement. But consensus on respect for our differences has.

14

THE FUTURE BELONGS TO US

We are convinced that the future belongs to liberal Christianity. Even though at the moment the Christian Right has the most public voice among Christians, ours will be the enduring witness in the coming years and will maintain credibility long after the Christian Right has faded into the background. We say this not because we are more deserving or virtuous, nor because the tide of public opinion is turning and momentum is beginning to run in our favor. No, the future belongs to us because history is on our side. The religious and political extremism the Christian Right represents has raised its ugly head before, and when it has, though reeking much havoc, it has consistently been exposed, condemned, and ultimately rejected. We believe this will happen with the Christian Right. What has been said of the radical right in general applies to the Christian Right in particular:

> They are on the wrong side of history, the wrong side of economics, the wrong side of technology, the wrong side of progress and the wrong side of the environment. These free-market fundamentalists are the people who regularly remind us that being in the buggy-whip business after the automobile was invented was a no-hoper.[1]

Contrary to what the Christian Right believes about itself, we are convinced most Americans will reach the conclusion we have already reached. They are "no-hopers" bidding our nation to return to a romanticized past while offering no way to move into the future. Liberal Christianity does. It offers hope for the future as it speaks a positive word about how faith and politics in this country can co-exist.

It will not happen quickly, of course. It takes an unusually long time for facts to impact the opinion of most Americans. The majority continues to believe, for example, that weapons of mass destruction exist in Iraq. One-third think they have actually been found. They also believe Saddam Hussein was behind the 9/11 attacks, even though President Bush has stated in public that there is no evidence such a link exists. For people who see themselves as the model nation for the rest of the world, Americans often have opinions that simply do not square with facts. At the same time, though, on the whole Americans tolerate extremism, but seldom embrace it over the long haul. The most strident voices have their fifteen minutes of fame, but then find that no one is paying attention to their outrageous claims. The Christian Right is currently enjoying its moment of fame, but if history is a guide, it will not win the day.

In a provocative article entitled, "Ways To Win,"[2] author Jonathon Schell makes the point that sometimes victory comes by a circuitous route. He notes that conventional wisdom holds that Democratic presidential candidate George McGovern not only lost the 1972 election to Richard Nixon by an embarrassing landslide, he lost credibility as well. Yet Schell argues that McGovern is correct in his recent assessment that because his campaign gave a national voice to the anti-Vietnam War movement, it would have been politically impossible for Nixon to continue it indefinitely. Thus, a "losing" campaign may have played a major role in ending the war. So, too, with the civil rights movement. Integration candidates in the South lost elections as the fight for racial equality was waged. But in the end it was the segregationist "winners" such as Alabama Governor George Wallace whose cause was lost.

We acknowledge that at the moment the Christian Right is more dominant than liberal Christianity, but liberal Christianity is far from dead. Indeed, it is the best hope Christianity in America has. The Christian Right is simply too radical, too unreasonable, too intolerant, and too extreme to have much of a future. We believe we represent perspectives on the issues of our time that will become the choice of most Christians. The issue of the separation of church and state is one example. The history of court rulings suggest that there will remain a "wall" of separation, to use Mr. Jefferson's phrase, that will prevent the Christian Right from realizing its agenda of prayer in schools and Christian symbols displayed on government property.

Despite the aims of the Christian Right, we are confident that public opinion will not grow to support them. Most Americans understand what is truly amazing about our founders. Against the backdrop of European models of government that blurred the lines between church and state, especially in regard to taxes and services, our founders established a secular government respecting religion but not promoting it. This extraordinary decision respected by justices across the political spectrum will prevent the Christian Right from having its agenda sanctioned by courts of law or public sentiment. That the Alabama Supreme Court colleagues of Justice Roy Moore, to whom we have previously made reference, voted to reject his position on the religious block of granite is itself indicative of why the future of the Christian Right's efforts to christianize America will fail. Even the current conservative leaning U.S. Supreme Count refused to hear Moore's appeal of the lower court ruling.

The mythological America the Christian Right has created gives them something to preach about, but constitutional law is not on their side and has not been since the 1940s. The first church/state case that went against christianizing schools took place in 1948. In Illinois vs. McCollum the Supreme Court ruled that religious teachers giving religious instruction in public schools was unconstitutional.[3] Since then Supreme Court rulings have been consistent in prohibiting the mixing of religion and public schools. The removal of prayers from public schools was a court decision that reflects the evolving maturity of American democracy every bit as much as the civil rights movement of the 1960s did when court actions again forced the nation to live up to its own Constitution.

The separation of church and state is not the agenda of "godless" liberals. It is the First Amendment to the Constitution, pure and simple. We believe future court rulings will continue to reject blurring the line between church and state. Even if Christian Right politicians win confirmation of their favorite judicial nominees, the tide will still not turn in their favor on matters of church and state. The past has shown that, more times than not, ultra conservative justices do not turn their back on the Constitution. Efforts to christianize America will not be put into law by judges who seek to do their duty to the nation as a whole. We believe that in the end separation of church and state will not be abrogated.

But we are not only counting on judges. We also trust that Americans believe in the virtue of tolerance, contrary to the Christian Right's contention that tolerance means anything goes and nothing matters except what feels good. The statement below is an amazing example of the Right's disdain for tolerance.

> Left to fester, tolerance and diversity, liberals' religion, will destroy America's traditional Christian church. Liberal socialists have spent years contorting diversity into a core virtue that demands goose-stepping acceptance of any value system, except founding American principles, without judging issues of right or wrong. Judgment used to be encouraged in America. Strong moral teachings and governmental structure, based on biblical Christianity, brought this country to incredible prosperity.[4]

The writer goes on to identify "kicking" Christianity out of public schools, whatever she means by that, is an obvious sign that tolerance is being carried too far. This, she believes, has led the nation to replace moral absolutes with a critical mind that rejects moral absolutes, and thus, Christianity as the purveyor of such absolutes. She argues that this has led to the mistaken belief that all actions and ideas are considered of equal virtue. This redefinition of tolerance, she concludes, "represents nothing less than a prime opportunity for revolutionary evil of untold proportions to flourish in America. You see, if nothing is wrong, we have no standards upon which to protect our children, elderly, families, churches and society."[5]

This is a point of view the majority of Americans now rejects and will continue to in the future, especially young Christians, as the Pew Research Center found in a survey regarding the relationship between religious beliefs and social attitudes.

> Over the past 16 years, public values on most social issues have remained generally stable. Eight-in-ten say they have "old-fashioned values about family and marriage," and nearly as many (77%) agree that there are clear and immutable guidelines about good and evil.

> The number who completely agree with these sentiments—about four-in-ten in each case—has shown only modest fluctuations over the past decade and a half.

> Yet in that period there also has been a distinct shift toward acceptance of several social changes, some of which challenge traditional views of the family. There has been a broad increase in at least limited tolerance of homosexuality—the number who believe that schools should not be allowed to fire homosexual teachers has risen from 42% in 1987 to 62% in the current survey.

> Nearly as striking is the growing societal acceptance of interracial dating…And there has been a more modest decline in the percentage who favor women returning to their "traditional roles in society" (from 30% in 1987 to 24% now).

> Consequently, an increasing number of Americans are able to accept such social changes as homosexuality and changing women's roles while maintaining traditional religious and social values.[6]

Liberal Christians find encouragement in such a survey of attitudes. We do not believe tolerance is inimical to religious convictions, nor are we convinced it is eroding the moral foundation of this nation. Indeed, from our perspective tolerance is not the problem. Intolerance is. More and more the Christian Right will see how "intolerant" Americans can be of their "intolerance."

Another reason we believe the Christian Right's light will grow dim as the future unfolds is the fact that while Americans are decent people who believe in justice and fair play, we are not really all that religious when it comes to practice, even among members of the Christian Right. Polls are consistent in showing that 95 percent of us profess to believe in God, more than 40 percent say daily prayer is important to them, and the majority now identify themselves with conservative beliefs.[7] What surveys do not reflect, however, is the fact that most Americans live lives that contrast the gospel they say they believe in. We are a nation of what theologians have for years identified as "practical atheists." In such a society it is not likely that the majority of people will support actions and laws promoted by the Christian Right that limit their freedom to live the way they want to without state interference. At the moment the majority of Americans do not believe homosexuality is "normal," but neither do they want police breaking into homes and arresting homosexual couples.

The problem with the Christian Right's effort to turn America into a Christian nation is that they major on minors. We do not believe the absence of prayer in schools or the Ten Commandments in judicial buildings matters much in how the nation lives. What does matter is how selfish and lacking in compassion we have become. We once asked ourselves during presidential campaigns. "Are we better off than we were four years ago?" Now we ask, "Am I better off?" In other words, how you are doing is no concern to me. This is a basic moral issue in America today. Selfishness rooted in an abject materialism is the real enemy of the nation's moral fiber. It's call "affluenza."[8] We see it manifested in numerous ways, none more telling than in professional sports. Pro-football is the primary example.

By far the number one fan sport, pro-football, is the focus of weekly worship. On Sunday, September 7, 2003, 1,095,720 tickets were sold by the National Football League. One game, the Washington Redskins/New York Jets game, drew 83,398 people. Millions more Americans watched games via television. In fact, on that same Sunday, 77 percent of all households in Minnesota watched the Vikings/Green Bay Packers game.[9] This is "sabbath day" for most Americans. Any sports worshiper has the opportunity to watch as much as ten hours of football on any given Sunday. In addition, many of them paint their faces and bodies, dress in team colors, buy cheap but expensive paraphernalia, and otherwise pay homage to the sports god whether they actually attend a game directly or vicariously.

Such devotion among the devotees of the God of Abraham and Jesus seldom runs this deep. The typical church member who actually attends a worship service in a church, on average no more than one quarter of those on the membership roll, grows restless before an hour has passed and indignant after the expected close of the service. This is the real world of America. Monday morning conversations are not about yesterday's sermon, the claim of God on one's life, or an opportunity to get involved in a service ministry of some sort. It is about the game the day before, or the golf match, or the marathon run, or whatever sport people happen to fancy. Indeed, there is more passion for Little League soccer than the God of the Bible any day of the week!

We take no comfort in this secularization of American life, but it does suggest that the Christian Right is living a fairy tale when it thinks it will force its moralistic will on such a population. The Thirty Years War that ravaged Europe in the seventeenth century ended when people got sick of fighting over meaningless religious differences between Protestants and Catholics and decided to go home. It wasn't as simple as Forrest Gump ending his run across America with the words, "I'm tired. I think I'll go home," but it had the same effect. Political and religious leaders would have gone on, but the people had had enough. The Christian Right will meet with the same fate as people say "enough" to what liberal Christians have already had enough of.

15

AN UNEXPECTED CALL FOR DIALOGUE

███

If our criticisms of the Christian Right have sounded harsh, it isn't accidental or incidental. Our views have been festering for years as we have listened to the Right baptize their political views and politicize their faith. We do not hate these people, though we wish they would accord us the same courtesy. We don't even want to silence them. We simply want to expose them. In doing so we have the faint hope, strange as it may sound, that speaking our minds could serve as an invitation to discuss our differences. Divisions within the church seriously undercut the Christian witness. How can we expect non-Christians to trust that we genuinely believe in the power of love when we cannot practice it among ourselves? The truth is, they don't, and they shouldn't.

Admittedly liberal Christians are woefully lacking in demonstrating unity among ourselves, but in the last century we have made great strides toward cooperation and mutual support by overcoming attitudes that feed division and animosity. There is a significant unity of spirit among us today that demonstrates the seriousness with which we take the words of Jesus: "I give you a new commandment, that you love one another. Just as I have loved you, you also should love one another. By this everyone will know that you are my disciples, if you have love for one another" (John 13:34–35).

We believe an attitude that says "my way or the highway" deliberately ignores these words of Jesus. If the judgment of God is as ready and quick as the Christian Right says it is, then Christians who pay no attention to divisions within the body of Christ will be the last ones to get in.

For this reason we are issuing a call for the Christian Right to join us at the table of dialogue. There has been too much straining at a gnat and swallowing a camel among Christians to be helpful or healthy. We are inviting the Christian Right to give up the notion that sitting at table with liberal Christians would be the equivalent of condoning what they believe is our apostasy of faith. There is no denying that serious differences exist between us, but we are at least open to dialogue that might make for an improvement of attitude on both sides. Just as we believe it is through relationships that barriers separating people are overcome, so we believe dialogue between us on homosexuality, abortion, war and peace, and other such issues, might build a relationship that can be the means by which the Christian Right and liberal Christians overcome their hostilities.

We do not believe saying this contradicts the challenges this book poses to them. Honest dialogue is rooted in honest differences. Unity does not grow from a refusal to state opposing views and perspectives. It is achieved when differences are put on the table. Contrasting points of view are not what separate people. Inflexible attitudes divide us. We could not be more determined in our opposition to the Christian Right's efforts, but this does not preclude our willingness to sit down and discuss the ways to overcome differences. Our attitude toward the Christian Right is not one of "you're either for us or against us." It is one that says we passionately disagree with you, especially when you tell us we are not true Christians. At the same time we respect the fact that you are Christians and we also respect your freedom to read the Bible as you do. All we ask is that you return the courtesy. We believe if the Christian Right is genuinely serious about witnessing to Jesus Christ, they will see the need for taking steps toward achieving better relations with liberal Christians. It is commitment to effective Christian witnessing that is at stake. They believe the moral fiber of the nation hangs in the balance. We believe the integrity of Christianity is on the line.

So to the Christian Right we say, "Meet us at the table, any table, in any community, and let us begin to identify what divides us and what does not." If liberal and conservative Christians have shared anything at all, it has been to allow fears to divide us instead of searching for common goals that can unite. The times in which we are living demand better from us than this, and we are willing to make the effort in this direction. But this will not happen without an intentional effort on their part to overcome attitudes that make them unwilling to engage us in this way. We do not have to agree on issues to have a conversation. Indeed, dialogue is needed precisely because differences do exist. But there has to be an attitude of openness to another point of view for dialogue, and from where we sit, the Christian Right comes up short in this regard. They need an attitude adjustment. No doubt they would say the same about us. Fine. We want to name the changes we think they need to make for dialogue to become a possibility. We welcome their suggestions to us, and would hope that ours might elicit such a response.

The first change in attitude we want to suggest to them is to recognize the essential distinction between being right and being christlike. This is not a liberal plea. It is, as evangelical scholar and writer, Dallas Willard, says in his book, *Renovation of the Heart*, a distinction that is the key to avoiding being mean-spirited in the name of Christ. Willard tells of a Christian college president who devoted his periodic mail-out to the question, "Why are Christians so mean to one another so often," and then quotes the president as saying:

> As a leader of a Christian organization, I feel the brunt of just this kind of meanness within the Christian community, a mean-spirited suspicion and judgment that mirrors the broader culture. Every Christian leader I know feels it...It is difficult to be a Christian in a secular world...But, you know, it is sometimes more difficult to be a leader in Christian circles. There too

you can be vilified for just the slightest move that is displeasing to someone.[1]

Willard believes Christians who believe being right is more important than being Christlike are likely to have the kind of mean-spirited attitude to which the college president was subjected. He even suggests that they are taught to act this way.

> Christians are routinely taught by example and word that it is more important to be right...than to be Christlike. In fact, being right licenses you to be mean, and, indeed, *requires* you to be mean—righteously mean, of course.[2]

Further, he says,

> A fundamental mistake of the conservative side of the American church today, and much of the Western church, is that it takes as its *basic* goal to get as many people as possible ready to die and go to heaven. It aims to get people into heaven rather than to get heaven into people. This of course requires that these people, who are going to be "in," must be *right* on what is basic. You can't really quarrel with that. But it turns out that to be right on "what is basic" is to be *right* in terms of the particular church vessel or tradition in question, not in terms of Christlikeness.
>
> Now, the project thus understood and practiced is self-defeating. It implodes upon itself *because* it creates groups of people who may be ready to die, but clearly are not ready to live. They rarely can get along with one another, much less those "outside." Often their most intimate relations are tangles of reciprocal harm, coldness, and resentment. They have found ways of being "Christian" without being Christlike.[3]

Willard identifies what is needed for dialogue between us and the Christian Right to be possible. We believe we are right on the issues that divide us. They believe they are right. What both of us also ought to believe is that being followers of Jesus rather than Jesus himself means that each and both of us can be wrong. To sit down and reason together in spite of what we believe would be to put our desire to be like Jesus before any need to be right.

The second change in attitude we suggest is for them to understand that liberal Christians are as committed to high moral standards as they are. We agree with them, for example, that explicit sex in movies and television does not simply reflect culture, but plays a role in shaping the culture. Further, we believe children and teenagers are the subject of intentional marketing of such shows and films without having the emotional maturity to view them. We are also concerned that important issues of fidelity and mutual respect among women and men are sometimes presented in a flippant manner that degrades the relationship they share. We do not condone illicit homosexual or heterosexual behavior, nor are we of one mind in how we view homosexuality. What we do agree on is the fact that hate crimes against homosexuals, or anybody else, are wrong and should be condemned by all Christians. The issue of abortion creates a similar kind of ambiguity for liberal Christians. The idea that liberal Christians support unrestricted abortion rights across the board is a generalization by the Christian Right with no basis in fact. That is the case with most generalizations, ours included, but we recognize that this is the case. We wish they did as well. But it is more likely the case that they do not, for one simple reason. They continue to want to oversimplify complex issues.

A case in point is a recent survey by George Barna & Associates purported to reveal people's views of what is morally acceptable behavior. The report carried the heading, "Morality Continues to Decay"[4] and began with a lead paragraph that said:

> Of the ten moral behaviors evaluated, a majority of Americans believed that each of three activities were "morally acceptable." Those included gambling (61%), co-habitation (60%), and sexual fantasies (59%). Nearly half of the adult population felt that two other behaviors were morally acceptable: having an abortion (45%) and

having a sexual relationship with someone of the opposite sex other than their spouse (42%). About one-third of the population gave the stamp of approval to pornography (38%), profanity (36%), drunkenness (35%) and homosexual sex (30%). The activity that garnered the least support was using non-prescription drugs (17%).

But does the report actually support the conclusion that "morality continues to decay?" A closer look raises serious questions about its reliability. For example, it separates evangelical Christians from all other "faith segments" by defining evangelicals as those who "believe that after they die on earth they will go to Heaven solely because they have confessed their sins and accepted Jesus Christ as their savior."[5] Moreover, the survey makes the broadest of sweeps in defining "other faith segments" to include "non-evangelical born-again Christians, notional Christians, adherents of non-Christian faiths, atheists/agnostics, and Protestants and Catholics," yet it does not name what non-Christian groups were surveyed. Moreover, the clear implication of the report is that all non-evangelical Christians hold moral views that reflect "decay."

As liberal Christians we would argue that the categories used to indicate moral decay are themselves controversial and have as much to do with a conservative agenda as they do with morality. Acceptance of abortion, for example, is considered a sign of moral decay, but the report says nothing about whether distinctions were made in regard to the views on abortion among those surveyed. Should someone who supports abortion within strict limitations such as rape, incest, or danger to the life of the mother be characterized as proving moral decay in American culture? The report raises the same questions about other indicators of "moral decay," and that is our main concern. These kinds of surveys are often used to support the agenda of the Christian Right when the results are anything but as simple as they are made out to be. Oversimplification in any form serves no useful purpose, and can stand in the way of honest dialogue about differences regarding controversial issues.

A third change in attitude on the part of the Christian Right that could open the door to dialogue would be to agree with us that Americans are a people living in servitude to the god of materialism that underscores the weaknesses of unbridled capitalism. It is not un-American or anti-capitalist to name the "demon" of runaway materialism as a consequence of the free enterprise system. It may be a necessary evil, but it is an "evil" nonetheless. It is, in fact, ruining the lives of millions of Americans. Bankruptcies are at an all time high, while the banking industry lobbies Congress for tougher laws to lower their losses that are the result of their own marketing of credit card materialism. Families join churches unable to contribute financially because they are up to the necks in debt. They don't just join liberal churches. They are in Christian Right churches as well. Surely this is a point of common concern between us that invites further discussion about what churches of all stripes can do to help people caught in the web of materialism.

A fourth change the Christian Right will need to make in attitude in order to be open to talking with us is to agree at least in principle that America is a religiously plural nation, requiring all levels and agencies of government to show respect for all traditions. Even though we disagree with one another regarding the intentions of our nation's founders, it is not asking too much for them to make an unambiguous distinction between believing the nation was founded on Christian principles and believing it was founded on the Christian faith. One can be an agnostic or atheist and agree with the moral teachings of Jesus while rejecting any governmental support for or promotion of Christianity or any other religion.

Respect for religious pluralism—including no religion at all—could serve as common ground between liberal Christians and the Christian Right. Democracy is not about protecting the rights of the majority. It is about protecting the rights of the minority. The fact that the Christian Right is so pro-American could, ironically, become a catalyst for a new understanding of the role of religious pluralism in this country. To support democracy means standing up for the freedoms of those with whom one disagrees. Therein lie the seeds of hope for an acceptance of religious pluralism to grow among those in the Christian Right. That, in turn, would make dialogue with us possible.

A fifth change in attitude would involve a rejection of an "us" vs. "them" view of the world. On an elementary level, no responsible parent would encourage her child to have this kind of attitude toward other children. Putting people into categories of conflict serves no worthwhile long-range purpose, even when it temporarily advances a particular agenda. What ought to encourage the Christian Right is the fact that the rejection of an "us" vs. "them" mentality has proven its benefit even in the business world.[6] Even when profound theological and political differences exist between them, Christians ought not to have to be convinced that "we" and "they" thinking is more consistent with the message of Jesus than "us" vs. "them." This is true for liberal Christians and it is true for the Christian Right. The view of the apostle Paul on this matter was unequivocal:

> Some proclaim Christ from envy and rivalry, but others from goodwill. These proclaim Christ out of love, knowing that I have been put here for the defense of the gospel; the others proclaim Christ out of selfish ambition, not sincerely but intending to increase my suffering in my imprisonment. What does it matter? Just this, that Christ is proclaimed in every way, whether out of false motives or true; and in that I rejoice. (Philippians 1:15–18)

It does not matter if the Christian Right thinks we proclaim Christ from envy, rivalry, or good will. We do proclaim Christ and, thus, the call in the text to drop the "us" vs. "them" attitude remains unavoidable.

A sixth attitude would be to acknowledge the fact that violence begets violence and that political policies that promote peace among all peoples is the only sane path for nations. The Middle East is an example of Palestinians and Israelis refusing to accept this reality. The one thing these warring peoples of a common heritage seem to have in common today is the belief that they can kill enough of one another to bring about peace.

It has not happened, of course, nor will it. The road to peace cannot be traveled by nations determined to dominate each other. Neither Israel nor the Palestinians admit that this is what they are seeking to do, but that is what they are trying to do.

The Christian Right seems to have a special interest in the Middle East as a fulfillment of biblical prophecy preparing the way for the return of Jesus. We say that it makes no sense to think a return of the Prince of Peace inevitably means war between Jews and Arabs. The Christian Right should be willing to join us in speaking with one voice to both groups worldwide that we believe peace is born of understanding and acts of reconciliation. There is precedent for this way of thinking already. Four former heads of Israel's domestic security service have publicly described Prime Minister Ariel Sharon's policy of retaliation and attack not only as a failure in bringing peace, but undermining the future security of Israel itself. According to the news reports:

> The four, who variously headed the Shin Bet security agency from 1980 to 2000 under governments that spanned the political spectrum, warned in unusually bold terms in an interview published Friday that Israel is headed for catastrophe if it does not reach a peace deal soon and that Israel must end its occupation of the West Bank and Gaza Strip.
>
> They also said the government should recognize that no peace agreement can be reached without the involvement of Palestinian leader Yasser Arafat and must stop what one described as the immoral treatment of Palestinians. "We must once and for all admit that there is another side, that it has feelings and that it is suffering and that we are behaving disgracefully," said Avraham Shalom, who headed the security service from 1980 until 1986. "Yes, there is no other word for it: disgracefully."[7]

When asked why they chose to speak out, the response was their "serious concern for the condition of the state of Israel," according to Carmi Gillon, who was Shin Bet chief in 1995 and '96. Shin Bet is Israel's dominant domestic security and intelligence service, with primary responsibility for the country's anti-terrorism efforts. Further clarifying their going public with their criticisms of Sharon's policies, Yaakov Perry, whose term as security chief between 1988 and 1995 covered the first Palestinian uprising asked the question, "Why is it that everyone—(Shin Bet) directors, chief of staff, former security personnel—after a long service in security organizations become the advocates of reconciliation with the Palestinians?" then answered "Because they were there. We know the material, the people in the field, and surprisingly, both sides."

This article underscores the fact that violence begets violence. Knowing that conflicts such as the Palestinian/Israeli one have no easy solutions should not cloud the judgment of all Christians in understanding that war is never the will of God and never the way of Christ. Perhaps there is such a thing as a just war, but it can never be "just" as long as it is a choice before all efforts in the pursuit of peace have been exhausted. It seems to us to be such a small request to ask the Christian Right to reject taking sides in disputes among all nations and join us in using its energies and resources to work for peaceful solutions to conflicts. Part of the way this can happen is for them to believe peace is possible and powerful. War is inevitable only as human beings believe it is. A fresh start in the direction of real peace in the world can be born of a basic conviction that it is possible. To believe it is and to reject the status quo today that says it isn't would be an important step by the Christian Right toward dialogue with us.

One last suggestion we want to make that is actually an underlying theme in all we have said is for the Christian Right to lose the judgmentalism that shows in most of what they say and do. We do not need to repeat the case we have already made for this charge against them. We want now to call on them to make a change, a turn about, in order to make it possible for us to engage in respectful discussion of our differences. Someone once observed, "The more one judges, the less one loves." Judging bears the fruit of condemnation of another while exalting one's self. Both stand in contradistinction to the way we read the gospel. Christians are not empowered to pass judgments on others or one another. We are called to love.

Indeed, our faith tradition says we must do better, for the sake of love. Thus, this call to Christian unity between the Christian Right and liberal Christians is a call to practice Christian charity toward one another.

If I speak in the tongues of mortals and of angels, but do not have love, I am a noisy gong or a clanging cymbal. And if I have prophetic powers, and understand all mysteries and all knowledge, and if I have all faith, so as to remove mountains, but do not have love, I am nothing. If I give away all my possessions, and if I hand over my body so that I may boast, but do not have love, I gain nothing.

Love is patient; love is kind; love is not envious or boastful or arrogant or rude. It does not insist on its own way; it is not irritable or resentful; it does not rejoice in wrongdoing, but rejoices in the truth. It bears all things, believes all things, hopes all things, endures all things.

Love never ends. But as for prophecies, they will come to an end; as for tongues, they will cease; as for knowledge, it will come to an end. For we know only in part, and we prophesy only in part; but when the complete comes, the partial will come to an end. When I was a child, I spoke like a child, I thought like a child, I reasoned like a child; when I became an adult, I put an end to childish ways. For now we see in a mirror, dimly, but then we will see face to face. Now I know only in part; then I will know fully, even as I have been fully known. And now faith, hope, and love abide, these three; and the greatest of these is love. (1 Corinthians 13)

Differences can exists where there is love, but apart from love, differences often produce judgmentalism. Liberal Christians do not live by the rule of love as we should, but we are at least committed to the effort. The Christian Right can show the same desire by simply listening to us instead of judging us.

If Bob Barr and the ACLU can join together in this way, it hardly seems preposterous to suggest liberal Christians and the Christian Right might be able to sit down to talk about how to bring an end to the public divisiveness that undercuts the goals either of us is pursuing in the cause of Christ on Earth. Warring Christian factions will never make the household of faith strong. We hope criticizing the excesses of the Christian Right will open the possibility of discussion that could result in a bridge replacing the barrier that now separates us. The one thing of which Christians on the right and left can be assured is that firing salvos at one another while refusing to sit down and talk is sufficient justification for the criticism that we do not practice what we preach. We can do better.

NOTES

▨

Acknowledgments

[1]Cronkite wrote this in a fund raising letter for the Interfaith Alliance, a non-partisan, clergy-led grassroots organization dedicated to promoting the positive, healing role of faith in civic life and challenging intolerance and extremism., after he retired as Host Anchor for the CBS Evening News.

Chapter 1   When Enough Becomes Enough

[1]Signed by the following clergy: Joseph Grubbs, Christopher Morton, Terry Steeden, Dennis Sanders, Mark McWhorter, Joy Linn, Jan Linn.

Chapter 2   Who Are They?

[1]*Slander: Liberal Lies About the American Right* (NY: Crown Publishing, 2002), p. 166.

[2]Pat Robertson, *The New World Order* (Dallas: Word Publishing, 1991), p. 261.

[3]In a twist of policies, Riley is advocating a change in the Alabama tax code that would shift taxes away from low incomes earners to the wealthy based on his belief that the Bible warns against oppressing the poor At the same time, The Christian Coalition of Alabama has been speaking out against the plan's tax increases. In an interview, John Giles, the group's president, had trouble pointing to a biblical passage that directly supported his opposition to new taxes, but he referred to Jesus' statement about rendering unto Caesar what is Caesar's. (see "What Would Jesus Do? Sock It to Alabama's Corporate Landowners" by Adam Cohen, *The New York Times*, June 10, 2003.) Pryor is a controversial nominee for the federal bench, and Moore has been embroiled in the conflict over refusing to follow a court order to remove a large piece of granite with the Ten Commandments etched in it he placed in the Supreme Court building two years ago.

[4]See her Web site, EagleForum.org and The Phyliss Schlafly Report posted on it monthly.

[5]Figures come from Americans United for Separation of Church and State based in the nation's capitol.

[6]Ellen Goodman, "No Crisis on The Federal Bench," Minneapolis *Star Tribune*, May 16, 2003, p. A25. Pryor has also "testified to Congress in favor of dropping a key part of the Voting Rights Act. In a Supreme Court case challenging the Violence Against Women Act, 36 state attorneys general urged the court to uphold the law. Mr. Pryor was the only one to argue that the law was unconstitutional. This term, he submitted a brief in favor of a Texas law that makes gay sex illegal, comparing it to necrophilia, bestiality, incest and pedophilia" (*The New York Times* editorial, Monday, June 23, 2003).

[7]Ibid.

[8]Ibid.

[9]Reported in the Minneapolis *Star Tribune* July 1, 2003, p. 5A, as having been first reported in the Israeli newspaper *Haaretz*.

[10]David Limbaugh, *Persecution: How Liberals Are Waging War on Christianity* (Washington: Regnery Publishing, Inc., 2003), p. 199.

[11]As, for example, a book by Richard Hughes of Abilene Christian College entitled, *Restoration Principles Reconsidered*, in which he argues for "new" epistemology of biblical interpretation that would lead the Church of Christ of which he is a part to rethink matters such as its position on women in ministry.

Chapter 3   Who Are We?

[1]Coulter, *Slander: Liberal Lies About the American Right*, p. 181.

[2]Ibid., p. 292.

[3]According to co-founder Gil Alexander-Moegerle in his book, *James Dobson's War on America* (New York: Prometheus Books, 1997), Focus takes in $100 million a year (p.33).

[4]Ibid., p. 185.

[5]Charles Kimball, *When Religion Becomes Evil* (HarperSanFrancisco, 2002), p. 1.

Chapter 4   Enough of Biblical Abuse

[1]HarperCollins, 1995.

[2]N. T. Wright, "Farewell To The Rapture," (*Bible Review*, August, 2001 issue online).

[3]Tim F. LaHaye and Jerry B. Jenkins, *Left Behind* (Cambridge, UK: Tyndale House Publishing, 1996). Twelve other titles have followed, all bestsellers.

[4]CNN broadcast on September 14, 2001.

[5]Ibid.

[6]Bob Simon reports, October 6, 2002, "Falwell Brands Mohammed a 'Terrorist'," CBSNews.com.

[7]Ibid.

[8]Ibid.

[9]Ibid.

[10]Ibid.

[11]Falwell made such a statement to a church gathering in Bristol, Tennessee, as reported on the web site, FalwellQuotes.

[12]There are leaders today who like Begin before them welcome support for Israel from the Christian Right. In the October 6, 2002, *60 Minutes* interview in which Falwell called Mohammed a terrorist, Bob Simon also noted that "Prime Minister Sharon can apparently trust the Christian Evangelicals to do the right thing too. They treated him like a rock star when they flocked to Jerusalem last week to celebrate the Jewish Feast of Tabernacles."

[13]Reported as part of the story and interview with Jerry Falwell by Bob Simon on *60 Minutes*, October 6, 2002. A transcript can be found on CBS.com, June 8, 2003 story entitled "Zion's Christian Soldiers."

[14]Ibid.

Chapter 5   Enough of Christianizing America

[1]The ADF is a Christian Right legal organization whose purpose is to counterbalance the legal influence of the American Civil Liberties Union (ACLU).

[2]The Alliance Defense Fund defines itself as "a national legal organization based in Scottsdale, Arizona. The Alliance is a consortium of friends and allies that support each others' legal work. The Alliance serves people of faith; it provides strategy, training, and funding in the legal battle for religious liberty, sanctity of life, and traditional family values." They believe their primary "enemy" is the ACLU.

[3]reclaimamerica.org

[4]Sermon by Jerry Falwell, July 4, 1976

[5]Sermon by Jerry Falwell, March, 1993.

[6]Moral Majority Report, September, 1984.

[7]The Jeremiah Project.com – http://jeremiahproject.com/index.html

[8]It was James Madison who wanted to protect the church from the state and Jefferson who wanted to protect the state from the church. But it was their common concern for the separation of church and state that led to the Virginia Statute of Religious Liberty which in turn became the basis for the First Amendment's Establishment Clause.

[9]They condemn Islamic terrorism, as we do, but refuse to condemn our own government's persistence in operating The School for the Americas, recently renamed the Western Hemisphere Institute for Security Cooperation that promotes terrorism in Latin America. They openly cheered at the fall of Saddam Hussein, but were silent about the U.S. having armed him to the teeth when he was fighting a war with Iran and turned its head for the same reason when he used chemical weapons against the Kurds in Northern Iraq.

[10]This especially concerns us in light of the recent release of documents revealing that the McCarthy era made possible because of a similar obsession with national security was worse than we even imagined. These government documents had been held for fifty years. They described the heretofore undocumented secret hearings McCarthy held during which he ruthlessly interrogated hundreds of Americans for being "suspected" communists.

[11]Stephen Carter, *The Culture of Disbelief* (New York: Anchor Books, 1994), p. 123.

[12]Ibid., p. 125.

[13]Ibid., p. 34.

[14]Ibid., p. 35.

[15]Ibid., p. 91.

[16]Reported in the Minneapolis *Star Tribune*, Monday, December 8, 2003, section A1.

[17]Carter, p. 93.

[18]Ibid.

[19]Carter offers a general discussion of religious exclusivism, pp. 90-96.

Chapter 6   Enough of Venomous Attacks

[1]Saturday, July, 2003.

[2]Reported by Brian Lambert's "Savage's meltdown burns his bridge," the Minneapolis *Star Tribune*, Wednesday, July 9, 2003, p. 7B.

[3]See *Slander* (op. cit)

[4]Townhall.com (January 18, 2001 and June 21, 2001 respectively).

[5]Ibid., Nov. 1, 2001.

[6]Ibid., April 25, 2003.

[7]New York: Crown Forum, 2003. This book makes *Slander*, her earlier attack on liberals, read like a Sunday school lesson. Reading *Treason* felt as if I was contributing to the career advancement of a woman who is suffering from either uncontrollable hatred or egoism, or possibly both. My only consolation is that I checked it out of the local library rather than buying it.

[8]Townhall.com, July 17, 2003.

[9]Spinsanity.com (July 5, 2003)

[10]Jefferson was a Deist.

[11]Posted on *The 700 Club* web site, Monday, July 21, 2003.

[12]David Brock, *Blinded by the Right: The Conscience of an Ex-Conservative* (New York: Crown Publishers, 2002), p. 135.

[13]This video was produced by radical neo-conservative Republicans who hounded the Clinton presidency for eight years with strong support from the Christian Right.

[14]The Christian Coalition web site is one example.

[15]Quoted in Brock's *Blinded by the Right*, p. 122.

[16]Ibid., p. 92.

[17]Ibid., p. 231.

[18]For more information on this club, read Michael Moore's book, *Stupid White Men…and Other Sorry Excuses for the State of the Nation* (New York: HarperCollins, 2001).

[19]Made on Robertson's *The 700 Club*.

[20]When the Dalai Lama was invited to speak to the Minnesota legislature in 2002, Lindner refused to attend because in his view Buddhism is "a cult."

[21]*The Minneapolis Star Tribune*, March 12, 2003.

[22]Lindner sights the book, *The Pink Holocaust*, a revisionist history book with absolutely no credibility, as the source of his "factual" claims.

[23]Quoted in *The Fighting Methodists* by Andrew J. Weaver; *Sightings* published by the Martin Marty Center at the University of Chicago Divinity School.

[24]Ibid.

Chapter 7   Enough of Baptized Partisan Politics

[1]Limbaugh, *Persecution*, p. 187.

[2]His comment was reported in Lynchburg, Virginia, and was conveyed to us by friends and family who live there.

[3]Alexander-Moegerle, *James Dobson's War On America*, p. 203.

[4]From the Interfaith Alliance web site, September 17, 2003.

[5]February 15 article on the WorldNetDaily web site.

[6]Robertson backed the Bush administration's challenge of the University of Michigan Law School's practice of using race as one criteria for admission.

[7]The suit stemmed from a 1998 incident in which Houston police burst in on the bedroom activity of two gay men based on a call from an angry neighbor who knowingly made a false charge that there was a man was "going crazy" in one of the men's apartment. Because of the law the men were arrested, spent the night in jail, and fined $200.

[8]A March 27, 2003 report.

[9]A March 24, 2003 report.

[10]A March 12, 2003 report.

[11]Ibid.

[12]Alexander-Moegerle, *James Dobson's War On America*, p. 203.

[13]Wendy Kaminer, talk delivered to Center for Inquiry–Metro New York, May 2003, and published in *Free Inquiry*, Oct/Nov 2003, p. 2.

[14]Ibid., p. 3.

[15]Ibid.

Chapter 8   Enough of Blind Nationalism

[1]*The American Heritage Desk Dictionary* (Boston: Houghton Mifflin Co., 1981), p. 639.

[2]From the time of the return from Babylon around 535 B.C.E. until the birth of Jesus, the Jews enjoyed only a brief period of political autonomy after the successful Maccabean revolt in 185.

[3]The story is found in Luke 4:16–30.

[4]The poll was taken March 13-16, 2003.

[5]Joseph Circioni uses this phrase in his analysis of Bush and his neo-conservative policies. See the Carnegie Endowment for International Peace web site.

[6]Jim Wallis, "An Open Letter To The Christian General," *Sojourners Magazine* on line at www.sojo.net (10-22-03).

[7]See Martin Marty's *The Righteous Empire* (New York: Doubleday, 1971).

[8]Jack Nelson-Pallmeyer, *Is Religion Killing Us?* (Harrisburg: Trinity International Press, 2002), p. 115. As Nelson-Pallmeyer notes, these events are now well documented.

[9]Ibid., p. 116.

[10]Ibid., p. 115.

[11]Manish Nandy, "A flag in the church," (*DiscplesWorld*, July/August, 2003), p. 44.

[12]Ibid.

[13]Ibid.

Chapter 9   Enough of Hypocrisy

[1]*The Nation* web site, posted May 15, 2003 (June 2, 2003 issue).

[2]In his book, *Falwell: An Autobiography* (Lynchburg: Liberty House Publishers, 1997), p. 320, he argues that the Lynchburg Christian Academy had no "whites only" policy or any intention of "circumventing integration."

[3]"Pat Robertson: His Liberia Deal," by Colbert I. King, Saturday, October 20, 2001; Page A27. washingtonpost.com.

[4]New York: Crown Publishers, 2002.

[5]Ibid., p. 185.

[6]Ibid., p. 216.

[7]A quote from Rush Limbaugh, p. 269.

[8]See Ramesh Ponnuru, "Values For Sale," and "The TVC Scandal: An Update, " NRO (nationalreviewonline), July 17, 2003.

Chapter 10   Enough of Historical Revisionism

[1]From Martin Luther's "On the Jews And Their Lies, On Shem Hamphoras."

[2]Steven Scholl, "Islam: a warlike faith," DisciplesWorld Magazine, April, 2002, p.5.

[3]Tarif Khalidi, *The Muslim Jesus: Sayings and Stories in Islamic Literature* (Cambridge: Harvard University Press, 2001), p. 3.

[4]Ibid., p. 5.

[5]Ibid., pp. 5-6.

[6]Ibid., p. 29.

[7]Ibid.

[8]Ibid., pp. 16-17.

[9]Ibid., p. 10.

[10]See the web site - www.fatwa-online.com – for numerous sites for informative articles on Islam.

[11]Ibid.

[12]Jailhouse Blues: The New Islam Remains The Same Old Islam," February 12, 2003, Free Congress Foundation Web site.

[13]Karen Armstrong, *The Battle For God* (New York: Ballintine Books, 2000).

[14]Kimball, *When Religion Becomes Evil*.

Chapter 11   Enough of the Persecution Complex

[1]Limbaugh, *Persecution*, p. 329.

[2]Ibid., pp.329-30.

[3]Ibid., p. 331.

[4]Ibid., p.332.

[5]Ibid., p. 334.

[6]Ibid., p. ix.

[7]Ibid.

[8]Ibid., p. 5.

[9]Ibid.

[10]Ibid., p. 30.

[11]Polls consistently reflect this percentage of Americans who claim to be Christian.

[12]Limbaugh, *Persecution*, p. 27.

[13]Ibid., p. 47.

[14]Ibid., p. 299.

[15]Ibid., p. 300.

[16]Ibid.

[17]From an interview presented in "Faith and Doubt at Ground Zero," PBS, *Frontline*, September 11, 2002.

Chapter 12   Enough of the Wrong Issues

[1]Al Franken gives a thoroughly researched argument that exposes how fictitious this perception is in *Lies (And the Lying Liars Who Tell Them): A Fair and Balanced Look at the Right* (New York: Dutton, 2003).

[2]In a follow-up program of *NOW* dated December 10, 2003, Moyers made reference to these objections and also noted that he had invited the media representatives on the show, but they had refused to invitation.

[3]As for example, Donald Carty, who resigned as CEO of American Airlines in April of 2003 when it was discovered that while he was ringing financial concessions from the union to stave off bankruptcy, he was hiding millions of dollars in bonuses for the American executives, including himself.

[4]Molly Ivins, "The Cock Roach Theory", December 10, 2003, *Dallas/Fort Worth Star Telegram*.

[5]From the PBS special on The War on Poverty, Spring, 2003.

[6]See *Falwell: An Autobiography* (Lynchburg: Liberty House Pubishers, 1997), pp. 320-21.

[7]"Private Schools Hit For Using 'Christian,' by Malcolm McGregor, April 13, 1967 *The Daily Advance*, Lynchburg, VA.

[8]*Falwell: An Autobiography*, p. 320.

[9]These are the same persons identified in chapter 1, note 1, as having signed the *Star Tribune* newspaper article.

[10]Reported in the Minneapolis *Star Tribune*, Thursday, September 25, 2003, p. A1 & A21.

[11]See any of the following web sites: The Christian Coalition, Jerry Falwell's, James Dobson's Focus on The Family, the Center for Defense and Justice, or the Alliance Defense Fund.

[12]Ibid.

[13]Reported in the Minneapolis *Star Tribune* May 1, 2003, p. A5.

[14]Census Bureau figures as reported in the Minneapolis *Star Tribune*, Wednesday, September 3, 2003, p. A6.

[15]Joe Conason, "Where's the Compassion," *The Nation*, September 15, 2003, p. 23. This article is adapted from Conason's book, *Big Lies: The Right-Wing Propaganda Machine and How Its Distorts The Truth* (St. Martin's Press).

[16]Ibid., p. 24.

[17]Vikings quarterback Dante Culpepper just signed a contract for this amount while owner Red McCombs continues to insist taxpayers should build his team a new stadium.

[18]This figures shows an increase of 5% in 2002.

[19]From an article they wrote published under the title, "The Universal Cure," *The New York Times* Op-Ed section, November 18, 2003.

[20]Ibid.

[21]Ibid.

[22]Ibid.

[23]Ibid.

[24]The Pew Research Center for the People and the Press, "Religious Beliefs Underpin Opposition to Homosexuality" Released November 18, 2003

[25]Ibid. The survey also reported: "Americans remain deeply divided over the essential cause and nature of homosexuality. A 42% plurality believes that being a homosexual "is just the way that some people prefer to live," no change from a Los Angeles Times survey conducted in 1985. But there has been a rise in the percentage who say homosexuality is "something that people are born with"—from 20% in the Times survey to 30% currently. The public also is split on the question of whether a gay person's sexual orientation can be changed—42% say it can, the same number disagrees.

"Still, most Americans say they are comfortable interacting socially with homosexuals. Just one-in-five say they are uncomfortable around homosexuals, while 76% say they do not mind being around gays. Highly religious white evangelicals are more likely to say they are uncomfortable being around homosexuals _ a third express that view. Even so, six-in-ten in that group say it does not bother them to be around homosexuals."

[26]The ruling was based on the fact that the court views marriage as a social institution that carries privileged legal status for child custody, survivor benefits, etc., and that denying such benefits deprives homosexuals of equal protection under the law. It also rejected the state of Massachusetts' argument that marriage is primarily for procreation since heterosexuals who cannot bear children can marry. The Court gave the legislature sixty days to rewrite the law to meet state constitutional muster.

[27]Reported in an article entitled, "Ruling will motivate both sides," by Shannon Brennan, *The Lynchburg News & Advance*, November 22, 2003, Lynchburg, Virginia.

[28]Ibid.

[29]Ibid. This statement was made by David Neumeyer, President of the Congregation, First Christian Church, Lynchburg.

[30]Ibid.

[31]See Ellen Goodman, "The Evolution of Marriage," *Boston Globe*, carried in the Minneapolis *Star-Tribune*, Monday, Novermber 24, 2003, p. A13.

[32]"The Power of Marriage," *The New York Times*, November 22, 2003.

[33]The Phyliss Schlafly Report, September, 2003, Vol. 37, No. 2, as posted in her web site, EagleForum.org

[34]Rep. Linda Boudreau, R–Farmington, Minnesota, has been quoted several times in local newspapers making this statement.

[35]To review the various sources of this information, see "Notes and Sources" in Michael Moore's *Stupid White Men…and Other Sorry Excuses for the State of the Nation* (New York: HarperCollins, 2001).

[36]John Isaacs, president of Council for a Livable World, in an article on the Council's web site, June 23, 2003.

[37]*The New York Times* editorial, Thursday, September 25, 2003.

[38]"The Earth Charter," Earth Charter–USA, Washington, D.C., a program of the Center for Respect for Life and Environment.

[39]Ibid.

[40]Ibid.

Chapter 13   The Liberal Christian's Manifesto

[1]"Seeker's Diary," Amy Gage, the Minneapol*is Star-Tribune*, Saturday, October 25, 2003, p. B6.

[2]Fletcher's book, first published in 1966, is no longer in print. In 1997, a new edition with an introduction by James F. Childress was published by Westminister/John Knox Press under the title, *Situation Ethics: A New Morality (Library of Theological Ethics).*

[3]Quoted in an article entitled, "What Color is God? Film helps revisit the question," by Samuel G. Freedman, reported in the St. Paul *Pioneer Press*, Wednesday June 25, 2003, section E.1.

Chapter 14   The Future Belongs to Us

[1]The exact source of this quote cannot be determined, but it is believed to be from a 2003 newspaper column by Paul Krugman, Molly Ivins, or Bob Herbert.

[2]*The Nation*, September 1/8, 2003, p. 8.

[3]See my book, *How To Be An Open Minded Christian Without Losing Your Faith* (St. Louis: Chalice Press, 2002), pp. 110-12, for a list of this and numerous other religion in public schools rulings.

[4]Laura Adelmann, "Diversity Plus Tolerance Equals Moral Destruction," *This Week* Newspapers, Burnsville Edition, August 9, 2003.

[5]Ibid.

[6]Survey results available on The Pew Research Center web site as of November 11, 2003.

[7]Ibid.

[8]Public Television produced a documentary on this "dis-ease" under the title, "Affluenza," in 1995, narrated by Scott Simon.

[9]Statistics reported in the Minneapolis *Star Tribune*, Friday, September 12, 2003, p. C13 and C4 respectively.

Chapter 15   An Unexpected Call for Dialogue

[1]Dallas Willard, *Renovation of the Heart* (NavPress, 2002), p. 238.

[2]Ibid.

[3]Ibid., pp. 238-39.

[4]Barna Web site, November 3, 2003.

[5]The report presents this definition in a negative way in that it identifies "notional Christians" as distinct from evangelicals on this basis.

[6]See James C. Collins and Jerry I. Porras, *Built To Last: Successful Habits of Visionary Leaders* (New York: HarperBusiness, 1997).

[7]Molly Moore, "Former Israeli security chiefs question policy on Palestinians," *The Washington Post*, published in the Minneapolis *Star Tribune*, Saturday, November 15, 2003.

Printed in the United States
39233LVS00002B/205-210